THE KINGDOM OF HEAVEN

IS IN YOU

DAVID D. WEL

Other Books by this author:
Fighting the Invisible Enemy; Know the Weapons of your Spiritual Warfare
Human Being as a Tripartite; Body, Soul and Spirit

Copyright © 2023 David D. Wel

ISBN: 978-0-6458195-3-3

No part of this publication may be reproduced, stored in a retrieval system, or transmitted, in any form, or by any means, electronic, mechanical, photocopying, recording or otherwise, without the prior permission of the publishers.

This book is sold subject to the conditions that it shall not, by way of trade or otherwise, be lent, re-sold, hired out or otherwise circulated without the publisher's prior consent in any form of binding or cover other than in which it is published and without a similar condition including the condition being imposed on the subsequent purchaser.

Cover design, typesetting and layout: Africa World Books
Unit 3, 57 Frobisher St, Osborne Park, WA 6017
P.O. Box 1106 Osborne Park, WA 6916

You will discover within you the Kingdom of heaven you thought was far away from you.

DEDICATION

This book is dedicated to the honour of the blessed Holy Spirit, who has blessed me with the knowledge, wisdom, understanding and deep revelations of the things I have written in this book. There is no one else I am prouder of today than he who has guided me to all the truth and has made my calling in this life abundantly clear to me. I am anointed by him to write many more books through his guidance now and into the future.

I am convinced that the theme of this book, and the deep revelations given to me by the Holy Spirit of scriptures, in the support of its main principles, truth, facts, arguments and examples will helped grow the faith of many believers and non-believers who will come across the book. I have no doubt that the book will reinvigorates Christians and enticed non-Christians, to rediscover themselves and particularly the God's parts within them.

You will rediscover the God you never knew was in you. Your spiritual senses will be activated and tuned in to the messages of heaven like never before. This book will forever change your thinking about yourself and the God you thought was far away from you.

TABLE OF CONTENTS

Acknowledgements ix
Prologue xi
Introduction xv

Chapter 1: The Lord Jesus Christ in You   1
Chapter 2: The Holy Spirit in You   51
Chapter 3: The Gifts of The Holy Spirit in You   65
Chapter 4: The Fruits of The Holy Spirit in You   106
Chapter 5: The Fear of God in You   138
Chapter 6: Your Body; The Temple of
       The Holy Spirit in You   151
Chapter 7: Your Soul; The Control Center
       of The Holy Spirit in You   170
Chapter 8: Your Spirit; The Communication Means
       With The Holy Spirit in You   194

Bibliography 253
How to Connect with Us 255

ACKNOWLEDGEMENTS

I would like to foremostly thank and acknowledge the contributions and efforts of my beautiful wife, Rachel Awuok Ayuel Mayen Kur, for always being there for me, as the rock and the strength behind everything I do, including the writing of this book. Her support with ideas, proofreading, editing, and especially the structuring of the title of this book, has been instrumental to me in the progress I have made so far as an author.

I would like to also acknowledge the efforts and support accorded to me by Mrs. Raelene Laurie Newall, who tirelessly does the editing, proofreading, and restructuring of the books, and has always produced wonderful results.

To you our wonderful supporters; we could not do what we do today without your continuous words of encouragement and your full support either; financially, socially, spiritually, and morally. It is my personal belief that I cannot succeed or do what I do best without the support of people. That is why I don't take you for granted in this journey of writing books. May the living God continue to give you more blessings as supporters of what is good.

PROLOGUE

At the onset, it is important to note that in this book, I will interchangeably use the terms, "man", "humanity", "mankind", and "people," throughout. You will notice that the New King James version of the Bible (NKJV), to which I will be citing and referring to in this book, often uses the word "man" when referring to human beings.

By no means am I trying to be exclusive to women or womanhood in my writing, however it is sometimes awkward to follow all the protocols of social and political correctness to be right in the eyes of many people. So please my brothers and sisters, understand my heart of inclusivity if you sometimes notice I use the word "man". "Mankind," means human identity in God for both-males and females, but the current world appeals of inclusivity and equality between men and women have taken it out of context verifying us through sexual orientations and differences.

In the same vein as well, I will in the book also sometimes interchange the terms, "kingdom of heaven" and "kingdom of God" to refer to the same thing although there is a slight difference. Here is the difference. Heaven is a place and God is the king of heaven. However, I prefer to use the term kingdom of heaven rather than kingdom of God, which is the title of this book. It is important to note that there is no issue with using either term, so long as it suits you.

Let's face it, and this could be the reason among others why many people missed the concept of the Kingdom of heaven. The Kingdom of God is not a physical Kingdom but a spiritual Kingdom. Certainly, when Christ returns to the Earth to rule as King, the Kingdom of heaven on Earth will becomes partly a physical Kingdom, but still primarily a spiritual kingdom, but as for now it is still a spiritual Kingdom. Many people who focused on the physicality of the Kingdom of heaven over spirituality of the Kingdom heaven, on Earth always get disappointed, because it is still fully a spiritual Kingdom that can only be accessed by faith now. This is also reasonably, why Jews got disappointed with the fact that the kingdom first appeared to them as a spiritual Kingdom, rather than a physical Kingdom. More than anything else they had wanted a physical Kingdom over a spiritual Kingdom-when Christ first came to the Earth. They had wanted a worldly Kingdom and the King that had to set them free from Roman's empire bondage and oppression and their cruel rulership over the Jews. This was the main reason among others that they had rejected the messiahship of our Lord Jesus Christ. Their expectations of the physical Kingdom were strongly rooted in hearts and their minds. To my biggest surprised through my own research studies, findings, and observations of many Christians and non-Christians alike on their position on the Kingdom of heaven, many people believe in physical Kingdom over spiritual Kingdom. To this effect it is of no wonder that this believe does not happen to the Jews alone, as we are also not exceptional today as non-Jews. Many people today want to see a physical Kingdom over a spiritual Kingdom. Unfortunately, there is no faith in what we can see and then believe. We cannot call it faith when we can first see things and then believe them. For now, God wants believers to access the Kingdom by faith as it remains a Spiritual Kingdom in this age. In the next age it will manifest fully on Earth as a physical Kingdom when the Christ returns to the earth again to rule the Earth with his Saints.

As for now the kingdom of heaven is an internal Kingdom that is based inside of you rather than outside of you. You cannot see it, but you can feel it. It is measured by internal righteousness, love, peace, joy, kindness, patience, mercy, compassion, and faithfulness among other things. When you have all these inside of you then you have the Kingdom of God. All of these cannot be found by individual effort unless you have the presence of God with you, in the form of the Holy Spirit. The presence of God in you can opens the supernatural doors of heaven from which the seven spirits of God can rest upon you. These are the spirits of knowledge, wisdom, understanding, might, counsel, and the spirit of fear of the Lord and the Holy Spirit, which are so critical for your knowledge about God. So, you can see the importance of seeking the kingdom of God first above all else. There is nothing on Earth you cannot do upon receiving these seven spirits of God.

On many occasions, many people, with myself included, focused on the by-products of the Kingdom of God - which are physical, material things. All the physical things come from the spiritual things. Things such as our families, jobs, education, businesses, thrones, finances, farms, and many other things of this world are least important in the Kingdom of God. You can almost have all these things and still struggle in life, because they are made by God, but are not of God. They are indeed important to you but not to God. All these things consume our time, energy, and resources, yet they have nothing to do with God. You can have these materials things and still miss God.

Matthew 6:33 But seek first the kingdom of God and His righteousness, and all these things shall be added to you. NKJV.

God knows, you need these material things, but he wants to see whether you will love him above the material things when he blesses you with them. That is all he needs from you and your heart. Do you worship things or the creator of things? I hope this will change your mind today about the material resources of this world. Before the Lord can bless us with material things, he must first bless us with spiritual things. Material things can more easily be lost than spiritual things. For example, if God has blessed us with long life on Earth, then that gives us the ability to enjoy all the material resources of this Earth. If God, has blessed us with wisdom then it gives us the ability to apply knowledge appropriately and impeccably to help many people.

INTRODUCTION

The Kingdom of Heaven for now in this age, is a spiritual Kingdom in you. It can only now be access by faith. It does not matter whether you are young or old, small, or great, rich or poor, free or slave, the Kingdom of heaven is in you. All you need is to wake it up in you. This book has come to do it for you. Whether you are a believer or sceptic that there isn't such a kingdom here on Earth, the truth is that such a kingdom does exist here on Earth. Christians and non-Christians alike must accept the fact that such a kingdom does exist here on Earth, but in the form of inner government and not a religion the way many people think, I must emphasise. This kingdom is not of the world but of heaven. Just as Earth is a place, heaven is also a place. Earth belongs to sons of man, but heaven belongs to God. Heaven as a place has a King and his name is the Living God. Heaven is led by a Godhead, God the father, God the Son, and God the Holy Spirit. Heaven also has angels, laws, systems, and policies that govern it.

God created the Earth purposely for sons of man, to rule, control and to dominate it on behalf of the Godhead. When mankind sinned through rebellion against God and sided with Satan, God withdrew his systems and policies from the Earth. Mankind was stripped naked of all the ruling apparatus of

Kingdom of heaven, including the Holy Spirit. Satan took over the rulership of the Earth from mankind. The Kingdom of Earth was established because of mankind's rebellion against God. Satan deceived Mankind and became the ruler of the kingdom of the Earth. God, immediately after the fall of mankind through the deception of Satan, had a planned redemption and restoration strategy in place. Obviously, Satan was never a good master to human beings, and because of his oppression and bondage against humanity, God had mercy, and the restoration of Earth to humanity began through his son Jesus Christ. During the times, God had left mankind with Satan on Earth, The Earth was influenced and poisoned with Satanic systems and policies of idol worship, immorality, injustice, bloodshed, hatred, murders, wickedness, deception, lying, blasphemy, and theft among other vices. The presence of these evils in mankind today indicate that the kingdom of Satan has not been eliminated from the Earth because of people who continue to reject God's restoration strategy (through Christ) and continue to side with the devil. Today, the kingdom of Satan or the kingdom of the Earth, continue to be represented by magicians, sorcerers, witchdoctors, astrologers, diviners, palm readers, psychics, spiritists, conjurors, demons, and Satan himself. However, upon Christ's returns to the Earth again this Satanic Kingdom will be completely removed from the Earth. The people who continue to represent this Satanic Kingdom on Earth will be judge and cast into the unquenchable lake of fire.

Contrastingly, Christ came to restore the original Earth to mankind through his death on the cross. He became the penalty of sins of humanity against God, to set them free from the bondage of Satan which was brought by the sin of rebellion against God. In short, Christ came to restore the stolen Kingdom to its rightful owners-the mankind. Through Christ, the heavenly systems and policies had to be reintroduced back to the Earth through mankind. The purpose of Christ was to reintroduce a spiritual Kingdom of heaven and not the physical Kingdom through humans, whose hearts and minds had to be reprogrammed through the kingdom of heaven's policies and systems. In reprogramming policies of heaven, this was the first message by Christ.

Matthew 4:17 From that time Jesus began to preach and to say, "Repent, for the kingdom of heaven is at hand." NKJV.

The first message of Christ was an appeal to mankind to repent of sins. To change the former ways of thinking and ways of doing things on Earth for the kingdom of heaven to come into a person. All of these had to be done internally and not externally. Christ came to destroy the work of Satan in mankind not outside mankind. The works of Satan are lying, magic charms, deception, greed, corruption, lewdness, violence, homosexuality, fornication, adultery, covetousness, witchcraft, divination, spell casting, extortion, sodomy, among other things. Literally, each human had to be reprogrammed from the inside through the help of the Holy Spirit to get rid of all these vices, and for the kingdom of heaven to be effective.

The kingdom of God on Earth is being led by the Holy Spirit. When we allow the Holy Spirit to live inside us, he will transform our thinking and hearts about the kingdom of heaven having a spiritual nature rather than being physical in nature. It is by doing so, that he will reveal to us the deep mysteries of the kingdom of heaven. This will be according to the grace and glory given to us by God, that we can feel within us, in the form of the holiness within our souls and spirits. It is a kingdom that once established within us, can never be moved. It is a kingdom that has great power and authority in the souls and the hearts of men and women of this world. The power and the authority of the Holy Spirit will give us the ability to preach the gospel, cast out demons, heal the sick, set the oppressed and the captives of Satan free, and win many souls to God.

I John 4: 4 You are of God, little children, and have overcome them, because He who is in you is greater than he who is in the world. 5 They are of the world. Therefore they speak as of the world, and the world hears them. 6 We are of God. He who knows God hears us; he who is not of God does not hear us. By this we know the spirit of truth and the spirit of error. NKJV.

The birth, death and resurrection of our lord Jesus Christ ushered in the new spiritual dispensation of the kingdom of heaven on Earth, from being a country, city, physical building, place, person, into the spiritual kingdom with the leading of the Holy Spirit, who lives inside us. The presence of the Holy Spirit within us gives our spirits the ability to commune with him who opens our spirit's senses to the supernatural world. The Holy Spirit will produce within you the nine fruits (love, joy, peace, longsuffering, kindness, goodness, faithfulness, gentleness and self-control) and nine gifts (wisdom, word of knowledge, faith, healing, miracles, prophecy, discernment, tongues and interpretations of tongues). Furthermore, you will have access to the seven spirits of God which are wisdom, understanding, counsel, power, knowledge, discernment and fear of the Lord. The Holy Spirit will also give you weapons of your spiritual warfare in the form of truth, righteousness, peace, salvation, sword and prayer.

The kingdom of heaven cannot be known by the natural human. The Bible refers to the natural person, as one who cannot know or understand the things of God because those things are spiritually discerned. Unless your spirit is awakened and your spiritual senses are also activated within you, you will never experience and enjoy the fullness of the kingdom of heaven in you. When your spirit is activated, you will feel or experience the kingdom of God through visions and dreams, words of knowledge, voice, law of conscience, prophecy, thoughts, and revelation. These are just a few ways and means from God, through which we can communicate with heaven.

1 Corinthians 2:12 Now we have received, not the spirit of the world, but the Spirit who is from God, that we might know the things that have been freely given to us by God. 13 These things we also speak, not in words which man's wisdom teaches but which the Holy Spirit teaches, comparing spiritual things with spiritual. 14 But the natural man does not receive the things of the Spirit of God, for they are foolishness to him; nor can he know them, because they are spiritually discerned. NKJV.

Now after you have allowed the Holy Spirit to live in you, you are no longer a natural man but a spiritual man. The three objectives of the spiritual man are to allow the kingdom of heaven to fully operate within, to develop a heavenly culture within and to help in the expansion of the kingdom of heaven into more territories on Earth. As kingdom of heaven citizens there must be a clearly developed culture within us that appeals to the people outside. Our main goals should be to produce a community of heaven on Earth that has language, lifestyle, values and morals that reflect the culture of heaven on Earth. Our priority should not be about going to heaven but bringing the culture of heaven to the Earth. The principles of the kingdom of heaven through us come with benefits such as power, honour, glory, and all heavenly blessings, that attract humanity to it. The kingdom of heaven within us will also set people free from the bondage of fear, discouragement, curses, poverty, hatred, sickness and hunger among other things.

The greatest decision you will make in your life is to accept the Lord Jesus Christ as your personal saviour in order to allow the Holy Spirit to live in you. This is a guarantee; when you accept Christ and allow the Holy Spirit to live in you, you will experience the full force of heaven in you like never before. There is no other claim I can make than this to you – God is as real as you. Never make the mistake not to believe in him. He is alive, and in him there is a life for you. Accepting the Lord Jesus Christ will be the greatest decision you will ever make in your life. Take it from me, you will never regret it. As a matter of fact, there is nothing you can do on Earth without our Lord Jesus Christ.

1

THE LORD JESUS CHRIST IN YOU

The biggest struggle many Christians are battling today is to believe that our Lord Jesus Christ is alive and can speak to us. One reason among others why people and particularly Christians cannot believe this, is that they think God's Kingdom is a physical Kingdom and not a spiritual Kingdom. They think that Christ came physically here to the Earth, died, and rose from death and when to heaven and promised to come back again physically into the world. But what is happening between the time he ascended to heaven and time he will come back again is not taken note of by many Christians. Yet he has promised in many scriptures that he will still be with us until the end of time. This begs the question, "How can a person who died and ascended to heaven, promise his "presence" here on Earth with those he had to leave behind on Earth, while he ascended to heaven, to come back later? This question cannot be answered until we bring out some facts and concepts and the characteristics of God's Kingdom here on Earth.

God's Kingdom has two facets, which are physical and

spiritual. This is how it is; Earth is a home of physical beings created by God including humanity, while Heaven is a home of supernatural Spirits. For spirits to function on Earth they need physical bodies. This is a law of God. To put it in context, when God created people, he created triune beings, meaning body, soul, and spirit. So, we are spirits with souls, who lives in bodies. What constitutes a true human being is the spirit part of us that was created in God's image. We know God is a spirit and we are also spirits. When man fell in the garden of Eden, God withdrew his spirit which made human spirits alive. Unless the spirit of God is within us, our spirits have no ability to communicate with God. There was a total breakdown in communication between God and mankind when mankind fell into sin in the garden of Eden. Humanity was left as a body with a soul but without a spirit. The immediate action which was taken by God, when he banished Adam and Eve from the garden of Eden, was the restoration of the spiritual part of His Kingdom back to humans, through our Lord Jesus Christ. This process immediately started with the son of Adam called Seth, and later came Noah, Abraham all the way down to Jesus. When Jesus Christ was here on Earth, the restoration of the spiritual part of God's kingdom was completed. After Christ's death, resurrection, and ascension, the Spirit of God (the Holy Spirit) was reassigned back to mankind. From this time, our ability to communicate with heaven spiritually was restored through Jesus Christ. I hope that this explanation has helped you understand the nature of God's Kingdom. Let us now go back to our point of discussion which is Christ in you.

Now the restoration of the Holy Spirit back to humanity gives us the ability to communicate with heaven today. This must be made absolutely clear without further confusion nor complication. We know God is a spirit, and we are spirits as human beings, so spirits can communicate with each other without problem. The reason many Jews and some Gentiles continue to perish today is the rejection of this fact. Jews were more interested in a messiah who was to restore to them a physical Kingdom rather than a spiritual Kingdom. In fact, they were looking for a powerful King who was to set them free from the bondage of the Roman empire. They were more interested in a physical King than a Spiritual King. Christ was more interested in restoring a spiritual Kingdom of God back to the entire nations of Earth than a physical Kingdom, to the Jews. It was never about the kingdom of Jews only, but the kingdom of God for all humanity including the Romans who were their oppressors. It was a kingdom that had to set free the whole of humanity from the bondage of Satan which was spiritual in nature. Jews never understood this agenda and as a result, they rejected the messiah. They continue to perish today while waiting for their messiah, even though the Roman Kingdom which was the cause of their oppression, was later dissolved. What they thought was their problem was resolved in the process and yet they continue to perish today. We are hopeful that God will restore them later before he physically comes back to the Earth.

The Spirit of God is the way in which we can access heaven. When the Spirit of God is allowed to operate or dwell within us, it gives us an opportunity to communicate with heaven very clearly. When this happens, our spirits are activated and can receive information from the Holy Spirit, including visitations to us by our Lord Jesus Christ. The only way we can know the things of heaven is through the spirit of God. The Holy Spirit is the important person of the Godhead who is assigned to us to handle our issues here on Earth. He receives the information from heaven and relays it to our spirits and takes the information from our spirits and sends it to heaven. When necessary, he arranges visitations by our Lord Jesus to us. There are many examples which many Christians and non-Christians alike have claimed, of the visitations of our Lord Jesus Christ to them. For example, my own wife Rachel Awuok, spoke to me about her own account of Christ's visitation to her in one of her dreams. Until now I make no claim of a visitation by Christ, but it is my sincere wish that our Lord may visit me one day. However, I have my own other accounts of interactions with the Holy Spirit. The Spirit of God has powerfully used me through revelations, dreams, and words of knowledge. I can easily interpret some of the Bible verses today which were once difficult for me, through the help of the Holy Spirit. Why is it necessary for Christ to be in you? The answer to this question is below.

COMMUNICATION

If Christ is in us, then he must communicate with us. The irony today is that even those who believe in Jesus Christ don't believe he can speak to them. This is a question those people must answer; How do you believe in Jesus Christ who does not speak with you? It is common-sense in the world that any relationship must be two-way traffic; we must speak, and people in communication with us must speak back to us. Well, I want to break it to you that Jesus Christ, even though he is in heaven, still visits us and speaks to us today on Earth. Many Christians today have their own personal testimonies of Jesus Christ appearing to them either in a vision, dream, through the bible, and prayer. This is not out of wild imagination, but Jesus clearly stated this in the bible before he left for heaven.

Matthew 18:19 Again I say to you that if two of you agree on Earth concerning anything that they ask, it will be done for them by My Father in heaven. 20 For where two or three are gathered together in My name, I am there in the midst of them. NKJV.

John 14:18 I will not leave you as orphans; I will come to you. 19 Before long, the world will not see me anymore, but you will see me. Because I live, you also will live. 20 On that day you will realize that I am in my father, and you are in me, and I am in you. 21 Whoever has my commands and keeps them is the one who loves me. The one who loves me will be loved by my father, and I too will love them and show myself to them. NKJV.

Revelation 3:20 Here I am! I stand at the door and knock. If anyone hears my voice and opens the door, I will come in and eat with that person, and they with me. NKJV.

Acts 9:5 "Who are you, Lord?" Saul asked. "I am Jesus, whom you are persecuting," he replied.

These verses from the bible plus many more indicate beyond reasonable doubt that our Lord Jesus Christ is alive and still communicates with us even after he is gone to heaven. These verses are exclusively for those born-again Christians who have devoted their life to him. When you seek Christ wholeheartedly, he will appear to you. As the last bible verse above indicates, Christ is looking for relationship with his friends and brothers and sisters. He promised not to leave us alone as Christians and when we hear his voice and welcome him in, he will come and dine with us.

Can I ask you this question; What do you think prayer is for? Whatever answer you may provide is okay, but this is what I think. Prayer is communication between us and God including our Lord Jesus Christ. When we pray, we are seeking God for a response to our requests. Pay attention to this because this is where the problem is, as many people want God to respond to them in silence. Silence means they don't want God to speak back to them but still want God to give them what they want. They want to see the results of their prayer requests from God, without God speaking back to them. Sometimes this thinking may be because of ignorance of the fact that God speaks to his children before or after their prayers. If this has surprised, you then you are not alone. I was one of those people who used to think this way. When things used to get difficult for me, I had to run to God in prayer and I expected the answers to my prayers, by God changing my situation, but without me hearing God's voice. I never knew that God could speak back to us after our prayers. This thinking is totally the opposite of what God wants from us, which is a response to us that must be well developed when we pray to him. God wants an intimate relationship with us. Before or after we have prayed to him, he wants to develop a personal relationship with us that is ongoing. God is looking for those he can trust, in order to perform great miracles and wonders through them. God wants us to develop a communication line through prayers, in order to reach out to other people through us. If we can provide our availability to God on a daily basis, we will see him do great things through us.

Interestingly as well, some people tend to pray to God directly without the name of Jesus Christ. Christ has stated very clearly that whatever we ask God we must ask through his, (Jesus's) name (John 15:16). Think again; could this be why most of many Christians' prayers are not answered? God can only answer prayers that are prayed through the name of Jesus Christ, his son. I will strongly suggest to you that you must invite the presence of the Holy Spirit and Jesus Christ himself before you pray. This is not only the right way to channel your communication, but also Jesus Christ is readily available to pray for us if we do not know how to call on God. Everything has been given to our Lord Jesus Christ by his father the Lord almighty, and if we want anything from God then it will be given to us through the name of Jesus.

Fasting is another way we can communicate with God. When we fast, we are disciplining ourselves by denying ourselves delicious foods and drinks for the sake of the Lord. When we begin to focus and pay attention to God during fasting, he is moved by our actions. Fasting is one of the important Christian rituals that brings us closer to God when we need him the most during difficult times. During a time of fasting, we are encouraged to read the bible, sing praises and hymns to the Lord while we engage him through prayer. While we fast, our revelation, knowledge and wisdom of God increase within us because we are not distracted by our daily routines. It is also an opportunity to study the bible in depth in order have better understanding of sometimes complicated bible verses that need the interpretation of the Holy Spirit. During fasting you are closer to God than you could imagine. Fasting moves us closer to God and in doing so the power of God is easily activated within us to defeat demonic spirits. Our Lord Jesus Christ recommends fasting to us if we are to have the power of God activated within us for battle.

Our Lord Jesus Christ speaks to us through visions. I may assume here, but I think most of the visions take place during the daytime while we are fully awake in the like of that one of Peter's (Acts 10:11-13). This does not mean that some visions do not happen at night; they do. What distinguishes a vision from a dream is that a vision occurs when you are fully aware of what is happening whereas a dream occurs while we are asleep. When you develop a communication channel between you and God, he can appear to you at anytime and anywhere. If there is something he wants you to do quickly, he can show you a vision of it to make clear what he wants you to do. Perhaps the greatest example of a vision, was the one of Cornelius and the Holy Spirit and Peter and the Holy Spirit. The Angel of the Lord appeared to Cornelius in the evening in a vision telling him to invite Peter into his home for an assignment from the Lord. When the Angel of the Lord departed from Cornelius, Cornelius called his two servants and explained to them what happened to him and sent two of them to Joppa where Peter was lodging. While the two servants were on their way to Joppa, Peter was praying on a housetop and saw heaven opened and an object descending to him, being let down to the Earth. It was amazing how God connected and facilitated the communication between the two men. Now Cornelius was a committed Christian, and he had done everything that was pleasing to God, but he needed a knowledgeable and experienced Christian like Peter to preach and to baptise him and his household with the Holy Spirit. You can see sometimes that God can be moved by our actions just as Cornelius was through the fasting and prayer, and his almsgiving to the poor. God cannot hold back if you do the right thing by him. All God wants are willing partners with him in helping people. Are you willing to be a partner with God today?

Acts 10:3-4,11-13 About the ninth hour of the day he saw clearly in a vision an angel of God coming in and saying to him, "Cornelius!" And when he observed him, he was afraid, and said, "What is it, lord?" So he said to him, "Your prayers and your alms have come up for a memorial before God. And saw heaven opened and an object like a great sheet bound at the four corners, descending to him and let down to the Earth. In it were all kinds of four-footed animals of the Earth, wild beasts, creeping things, and birds of the air. And a voice came to him, "Rise, Peter; kill and eat." NKJV.

In addition, the Bible is the book that God uses to communicate to us. But if the truth be told, the Bible continues to challenge many Christians because of their lack of knowledge and understanding of it. This is due to the comparative, metaphoric, figurative, and poetic language used. This has led to misrepresentations and misinterpretation of its words from their true meanings. Think about it; there is no area of our lives that the bible has not addressed and answered. The only thing we lack is the understanding of its contents. It is the only book that has survived all years and generations of people of the Earth. Upon understanding the words in the bible as truth and life, you may be a winner against Satanic principalities and powers. The words in the bible are true words of God written by men filled by the Spirit of God. So, they are God's. They were written to help us in all our situations. They were written to give us knowledge and understanding of the invisible God. Next to the blood of our Lord Jesus Christ are his words, which the Devil fears. You see the Devil knows it better than us that the words of the bible are life, and if we apply them in our daily defence against him, he will never stand a chance to defeat us. That is why he has to make sure that you do not come near the bible and when you do, he will make sure that you do not understand it. There is an illogical and irrational argument that the bible was written by humans. When I come across people who believe this, I ask them this question; what is it that was not written by men? This argument is a lie from the pit of hell and the Devil himself. The only way you can have knowledge of God is through the word of God. Even if you develop other sources of communication with God, the bible is still important for confirmation and reference.

Nonetheless even if many Christians have developed other ways of communicating with God, one thing they still fear is the voice of God. And I do not blame them, because sometimes, when you claim to respond to the voice of unseen Spirits, many people may perceive you as mad or crazy. However, I strongly advise you to isolate when you immediately hear the voice of the Lord speaking to you. When you hear his voice, never put it aside for another day, because God loves it when you respond to him immediately.

Because any delayed response to the voice of the Holy Spirit, may be considered by him as an act of disobedience. For example, just in the case of Cornelius and Peter mentioned above, he may have an immediate assignment for you. Imagine if Peter had delayed, the people who were baptised on that day would have dispersed from Cornelius's house. It may serve as a warning for an immediate danger that he wants you to avoid. When you become a friend of God, he can protect you twenty-four hours a day. His eyes are always on you. It is important also to note that his voice may vary, as it may be a voice outside us or a still inner voice within us. God has used this a lot for me. Every day when I wake up from my sleep, I first pay attention to the inner voice and the outer voice in the environment around me. Let me tell you about my personal experience with this voice of God. There was one day I attended a function, and the function lasted until 3:00 a.m. in the morning. When the function ended and I was about to leave, I normally choose either of two ways to travel back to my house. Because it was the middle of the night it was difficult for me to choose which way to go as one way was very risky at night, yet the shortest to my house while the other way one was further yet safe both at night and day. As human instinct would always dictate, I chose the short risky way to my house, and while I was travelling on it, the voice of the Holy Spirit came upon me, very powerfully instructing me not to travel on it and instead take the longer route back to my house. I decided not to listen to his voice and continue traveling on the road, and he warned me three times not to do it, then he was silent. I continued traveling on the road, and while approaching some traffic lights, I saw a crowd of people disappearing into the distance. While I was still far from the traffic, my eyes could not distinguish between the Police and the people. As I approached the traffic lights, I began to recognise the people at a reasonable distance, and it became clearer to me that there was a heavy presence of police busy dispersing the crowd. As I stopped at the traffic lights, there was blood on the ground everywhere. I looked towards the police where there were many people, and saw injured people standing around an ambulance, as there had been a fight there Immediately, it came to my mind that this was the incident that the Spirit of God had wanted me to avoid. Either way we must always listen to the voice of the Spirit of God, because he knows it all. This is a good example of why the living God wants to be our friend and to talk to us daily, in order to avoid the traps and dangers of this world that Satan may put upon us. Make him your friend and you will see the wonders of the living God, within and for you.

Dreams are the best way God talks to us. I call them the best way, because no one can deny the fact that they have dreamed, or they can dream. This is because dreams occur at night when everything around us is silent. People can deny other ways of which God can communicate to us, but no one can deny that they can dream. God has designed it this way that we can hear him clearly and without the distractions that normally happen during the day. It would be unusual for people to deny the fact that they can dream dreams. If we agree that we can dream dreams, then who do you think talks to us in a dream, if it is not God or Satan? Because we are actively engaged with our daily happenings during the day, the spirits can be ignored by us unless we have full knowledge of God's voice. Many people ignore God's voice during their dreams, and they still wait for God to tell them what to do. God can appear to anyone in a dream of a night whether they are children, elders, men or women, Pastors and young or old. A good example of this is perhaps Joseph (Genesis 37:7/9). God began to develop his personal relationship with Joseph at a very young age through night dreams. God appeared to him in one of his dreams at night, of what Joseph would later become by showing him the sun, moon and stars bowing down to him. Because he was young and inexperienced, he went and told his father (who was an expert in interpreting and understanding dreams), what he saw in the dream. His recklessness in spreading what he saw in the dream to the rest of the family members became the source of the enmity between him and his brothers. Obviously, his father was also not happy with what God had shown Joseph in a dream, but did nothing to him, yet his brothers over time planned evil in their hearts and monitored him, and when an opportunity came, they dropped him into a pit. Later they brought him out of the pit after their disagreement over the harshness of their action and sold him to some merchants from Egypt. Off he went to Egypt, not to been seen by his family again for a while because of his dreams. What does this tell you? That our dreams are a true source of communication between us and the living God. Our dreams can be a true source of our assignment from God. In addition, we must be careful with what we received from God because it can cause enmity between us and the people around us. Furthermore, if we pay attention to our dreams, God could be giving us our entire life assignment, like he did for Joseph. Joseph became great because of the assignment God showed him at his young age. God still speaks to us today through dreams, in fact he has promised this in the book of Acts, particularly for the end time we are in now.

Acts 2:17-19 'And it shall come to pass in the last days, says God, That I will pour out of My Spirit on all flesh; Your sons and your daughters shall prophesy, your young men shall see visions, your old men shall dream dreams. And on My menservants and on My maidservants I will pour out My Spirit in those days; And they shall prophesy. I will show wonders in heaven above and signs in the Earth beneath: Blood and fire and vapor of smoke. NKJV.

JESUS CHRIST IN YOU, AS THE WAY TO GOD

The relationship between God and humans was restored through Jesus Christ. Humanity's way back to God, the truth of God and the life of God was restored through the blood of Jesus Christ, used as the atonement for mankind's sins committed in the garden of Eden. Since the garden of Eden rebellion by Adam against God, and before Jesus Christ came to the world, humanity lived on Earth without knowledge of God as the way, truth, and life. Humanity had totally lost the way of God until Christ came on to the scene. Even those who had claimed to know the way, truth, and life of God (such as Pharisees, Sadducees and scribes), were later proven wrong by our lord Jesus Christ, that they knew nothing about God and his ways. The Bible says, if they had known him, they wouldn't have crucified the lord of glory (1 Corinthians 2:8). Why would you crucify someone who came to set you free from the bondage of Satan, if you knew God? This was a complete hypocrisy and blindness from the Pharisees, Sadducees and scribes. So, the prominent people of Israel at that time, knew not about the way, truth and life of God. Let me now talk about the importance of the way and the person who directs us.

Common sense tells that in ideal world situation you will never travel to a home, place, or city without first seeking how to get there. Otherwise, if you just embark on that journey, you are most likely going to be lost. You must seek the means to find the way to get there and to get there very quickly. This is common sense for very man and woman who wants to travel. If you are in the western world, then you will find and use a street directory or GPS to get you to the place or the city you want to visit. If you are in the developing world, you will use people who have the knowledge about the place you want to travel to. They must explain to you very clearly the shortest way possible to the place in order not to get lost on the way. You can see how important it is to know the way to a place you want to go in the natural world. What about the way to God's place (heaven); don't you think you have to be shown the way? Well, you do. Even though our lord Jesus Christ's disciples had lived with him, they never knew the way to God. In fact, some of them never knew Jesus as the son of God and as God, as well. Even those disciples never knew the way, yet they had been with him three and a half years. Unless God shows us the way we will never know the way to him.

John 14:4 And where I go you know, and the way you know." 5 Thomas said to Him, "Lord, we do not know where You are going, and how can we know the way?" 6 Jesus said to him, "I am the way, the truth, and the life. No one comes to the Father except through Me. 7 "If you had known Me, you would have known My Father also; and from now on you know Him and have seen Him." 8 Philip said to Him, "Lord, show us the Father, and it is sufficient for us." 9 Jesus said to him, "Have I been with you so long, and yet you have not known Me, Philip? He who has seen Me has seen the Father; so how can you say, 'Show us the Father'? 10 Do you not believe that I am in the Father, and the Father in Me? The words that I speak to you I do not speak on My own authority; but the Father who dwells in Me does the works. 11 Believe Me that I am in the Father and the Father in Me, or else believe Me for the sake of the works themselves. NKJV.

Jesus Christ came to show us the way back to God. I must stress that this is a spiritual way not a physical way. It is important to have this at the back of your mind. The spiritual dispensation was ushered in when Christ was crucified on the cross allowing the Holy Spirit to return to mankind. While Christ was here on Earth his spiritual body was limited by his human body and couldn't be present everywhere at the same time. However, he had taught those who were around him the way of God and left the rest to the Holy Spirit. Immediately when Christ left, the Holy Spirit took over his role and he is now present everywhere in born-again Christians across nations, to those who have given, and continue to give him room in their hearts. The Spirit of God has the knowledge of the way to God and works through the men and women who have given themselves up to be used by him to teach other men and women the way of God. Amongst these men who were filled by the Holy Spirit and assigned to teach the gospel to the Jews and to the Gentiles were St Peter and St Paul; St Peter to the Jews and St Paul to the Gentiles. If you want to know God better, then the bible shows the clear way to God, with the help of the Holy Spirit. You must read it daily, and it will become clearer to you day by day with help of the holy spirit. The bible was written by men and women filled with the Holy Spirit and it must also be taught by men and women filled with the holy spirit.

Many people of the world have come up with many ways to God today through many religions, but none of those ways is true if it rejects the bible as the word of God and rejects Jesus Christ as the son of God. This is how quickly you can tell the false Church and the false religion. We must be careful about the religions of the world including our Christian faith, as there are now many ways, doctrines, and rules developed by men and women that are contrary to bible teachings, and which also reject Jesus Christ as the son of God. Amongst these are the leading religions of the world today such as Islam, Hinduism, Buddhism and Confucianism. Also, some religions such as Jehovah Witness and Mormonism, reject Jesus Christ as the son of God. And so there is no way to God among these religions. If you are in one of these religions and you want to have eternal life, then you must leave immediately. The only church you should belong to is the church that acknowledges the existence of the Holy Spirit, Jesus Christ and God almighty. The absence and the lack of acknowledgements of the Godhead in a church means that the church does not know the way to God.

JESUS CHRIST IN YOU, AS A TRUE GOD

Truth is fact-based evidence about a matter, or it is what many people believe to be true of a matter. What you believe about a matter, remains the truth to you until other information comes in challenging your previous belief about the matter, which you had deemed truthful. Now the information that remains unchallenged about the matter remains in your mind as the truth. That is why as Christians we have an obligation not to believe everything to be truth until we have examined the facts, evidence and principals governing the matter. The only template we must refer everything to when we are faced with new truth, is the bible. If the truth being purported is not supported by the bible, then it is a lie, or you may seek the interpretation of the Holy Spirit over the matter.

We as Christians must admit this truth about Christ, that he is God and man at the same time. He was God before he became a man. After he died, he returned to being God. He became a man to defeat the sins of the flesh which humanity had no power to defeat because of Satan who had power over death. Sin brought death on humans and humans couldn't live without sinning, giving Satan power of the spirit of death that activated sins. So God had to get himself a body to come and get rid of sins in the flesh on behalf of mankind. What a wonderful love from God almighty. Jesus Christ existed in the spirit as God before he became a man. There is no other book of the bible which proves this more than the book of John the gospel.

John 1:1 In the beginning was the Word, and the Word was with God, and the Word was God. 2 He was in the beginning with God. 3 All things were made through Him, and without Him nothing was made that was made. 4 In Him was life, and the life was the light of men. 5 And the light shines in the darkness, and the darkness did not comprehend it. NKJV.

If you cannot believe this, then you will never believe any truth about the deity of Jesus Christ. Before Christ was, no man or woman had the ability to predict Jesus' death, resurrection and ascension to heaven. He was born purposely to establish the Kingdom of God on Earth through men and women who believe in him. Men and women would come to accept this truth about the mission of Christ on Earth. He was crucified because of this truth, when he called himself the son of God and King of Jews. This was the reason why he was born. **When Pilate asked him, "Are you King of the Jews?" He responded, "You say that I am a king. For this purpose, I was born and for this purpose I have come into the world, to bear witness to the truth. Everyone who is of the truth listens to my voice." (John 18:37).** Jesus Christ is the truth and there is no lie in him. You had better believe in his mission. Be part of the Kingdom on Earth. We are all capable of knowing and believing the truth and none of us can refer to ourselves to be the truth. The reason is that none of us knows everything and even those things that we know, we do forget very quickly if we are not reminded. Hence, we have no ability to be the truth and to judge the truth. I must repeat this again, his entire mission of being born a man and living life as a man was to defeat Satan on our behalf and to establish the Kingdom of heaven on Earth through us and all mankind. This is the truth you must believe and stick with for the rest of your life. If you want to live, then you must believe this truth. If you want to defeat Satanic attacks, then you must believe this truth. If you want to defeat death, then you must believe this truth.

Hebrews 2: 14 Inasmuch then as the children have partaken of flesh and blood, He Himself likewise shared in the same, that through death He might destroy him who had the power of death, that is, the devil, 15 and release those who through fear of death were all their lifetime subject to bondage. 16 For indeed He does not give aid to angels, but He does give aid to the seed of Abraham. NKJV.

There are many truths in the world today working and competing against this true nature of God, in Christ. Our Lord Jesus Christ became a man to reconcile mankind back to himself and particularly about the origin of mankind. He came to the Earth to defeat sin in the flesh that had given Satan power to kill human beings through their sinful nature. There are many scientists who have developed their own truth about the origin of humans. Scientists like Charles Darwin, and his theory of evolution stated very clearly that mankind evolved from monkeys. I want to categorically state that this is absolutely a lie. God stated very clearly in Genesis 1:26, that he created humans in his own image. We know God is a spirit and so we are spirit. He also created animals and plants to produce after their own kind. This version of creation by scientists plus other versions of creation in traditions, cultures and religions of the world distort the truth of God about your origin as a person. This is completely the work of Satan to deny you your own salvation from God. It is up to you, which version to believe, God or Satan.

Genesis 1:26 Then God said, "Let Us make man in Our image, according to Our likeness; let them have dominion over the fish of the sea, over the birds of the air, and over the cattle, over all the Earth and over every creeping thing that creeps on the Earth." 27 So God created man in His own image; in the image of God He created him; male and female He created them. 28 Then God blessed them, and God said to them, "Be fruitful and multiply; fill the Earth and subdue it; have dominion over the fish of the sea, over the birds of the air, and over every living thing that moves on the Earth." NKJV.

CHRIST IN YOU AS A SOURCE OF YOUR LIFE

This is my favourite area of discussion, because of this; since humans fell into sin from the garden of Eden, they have no ability to save themselves from death. Before Christ's death and resurrection, no man or woman had the ability to rise from death. Until God came in the form of man, humans had no power to defeat Satan. In the garden of Eden humanity fell prematurely before they acquired the characteristics of the spirit, including the ability to live forever. God was preparing Adam and Eve to become like himself, and they fell before having the possibility of living forever. The reason why Satan has dominance over humans is their fear of death. Once Satan has killed the body, he has no power over the spirit which is our true self. Once you know this as a person, Satan will never have dominance over you and your family. He is a defeated foe who is just threatening you with things of the body. But when you are dead, he has no power over you, but God has. It is God who decides where you go after you are dead, whether to heaven or hell. If you know this, then you will never waste your time worshiping Satan. Satan together with the spirit of death will be destroyed by God when the final judgement of all things of this world take place. This world will be judged by our Lord Jesus Christ and that is one of the reasons we preach to men and women to avoid the coming judgment.

Because man has no life in himself, it is only God who can gave him life. This is indicated by the fact that we just die at any time whether we are young or old without our permission and against our will; death comes suddenly on us. Whether it is life here on Earth or the eternal life that is to come we must commit ourselves to God. Without God in our lives, we are in total darkness. The life of God is the light of humanity. Christ is the life of mankind. He gave his own life for the sake of our lives in order for us to live forever. He did so because he had the ability to live again after his death on the cross, and subsequent resurrection. He died and arose again from the dead to prove to men and women who will believe in him, that there is life after death. He first descended to hell to prove to us that there is hell and He ascended to heaven openly to prove to us that there is heaven. Either way we will live in one of those two places when we die. Remember we are not bodies we are spirits and spirits don't die; they join the other spirits in the spiritual world.

Christ has left us with the holy spirit to teach us about the things of heaven. Therefore, there is a need for you to be born again through the Holy Spirit. When you are born again by the spirit, you can have the knowledge of the things of God because you have become a legitimate child of God. Unless you have the spirit of God in you there is no way you can become a son of God. It is crystal clear as spring water. There is no way you can know the things of God without the spirit of God. With the life of our Lord Jesus Christ, God has accepted us back to himself and has given us his spirit as a seal of our salvation. We have been given a chance again to live this life, mindful of the life to come so that we do not lose it again just as Adam did. Before Christ, no man or woman had the ability to rise from death, let alone go to heaven. God through Christ had to reverse this; instead of going to hell, people who believe in him will go to heaven. People who continue to go to hell now are those ones who have rejected Christ as the source of their salvation and by doing so they send themselves to hell. Your life is hidden with Christ, and you must seek the things above not things on Earth. Everything that is seen was created out of those things that are not seen. Heavenly things are far better than Earthly things. Everything which you see on Earth is being controlled in heaven; you may crave for them, but it will be in vain without the permission of God.

Christ is the solution to all your problems. To those who are rejecting our lord Jesus Christ and his works, it is okay to do so but remember this; he holds the keys of life, death and hell. So long as you continue to commit sins you will continue to die for your sins. There is no other solution outside of Jesus Christ. God has given him to us as the atonement for our sins. Think again. Jesus was betrayed, humiliated, spat on, ridiculed, despised, stricken, denied and forsaken, above all for you to come back to God. Never let this opportunity of grace go without accepting him before the door is supernaturally closed.

AS BORN-AGAIN CHRISTIANS WE MUST BE IN CHRIST, IN ORDER TO BE FRUITFUL ON EARTH

The ability to be in the spirit is not through our bodies and souls but through our spirits that are born of the spirit of God. The ability to know the things of the spirit is not through our human bodies and human souls, it is through our human spirits. I cannot emphasise this enough; God is a spirit and those who would want to live and work in the spirit, connect through his spirit. Our lord Jesus Christ put it very clearly in these verses of the bible.

John 15:5 I am the vine, you are the branches. He who abides in Me, and I in him, bears much fruit; for without Me you can do nothing. NKJV.

Using the analogy of the vine or the tree here, Christ is saying that it is impossible for the branches of the tree to survive on their own without the tree itself. What holds the branches of the tree together is the tree. All the branches of the tree are dependent upon the whole tree for food, water and to grow. Let's get to the real business; what does Christ mean by using this analogy? Christ means that the ability for every

Christian to survive is through him alone. Christ is the life and has the ability give life to us through his spirit. Human beings have no ability of their own to sustain themselves, let alone have life independent of God. In as much as he was speaking to his disciples who were by then growing in numbers, to abide in him as branches, he is still speaking to us today to abide in him. Whether it was preaching the gospel, healing the sick, speaking in tongues or casting out the demons, none of these things could be done by the disciples without the Holy Spirit of God. When we are in Christ, we can qualify for the grace of God which gives us the ability to perform miracles, preach the gospel and pray for the sick. We must maintain close connection with Christ to communicate, grow, multiply and be fruitful, for our holiness, strength, and perseverance.

Christ is very clear that we can do nothing without him. There is no way we can know and understand the things of the spirit unless we allow the spirit of God to work through us. Things of the spirit are spiritual, and they can only be known through the spirit. Things concerning our exercise of grace, work, and strength to carry on with what we do daily, cannot be done without the spirit of God or just by our free will. We cannot just wake up every day to heal the sick, preach the gospel and perform miracles and cast out demons without the spirit of God. It is impossible. No demon will ever run away from us without sensing and acknowledging the presence of the spirit of God within us. There is no good work a man or woman can do without the presence of the Spirit of God with them. You cannot think well, speak well, and do good things without the spirit of God. The ability to do good things by ourselves is not given to us by God.

John 15:7 If you abide in Me, and My words abide in you, you will ask what you desire, and it shall be done for you. NKJV.

In this verse it goes up to the next level. Now if you abide or remain in Christ as a branch you can do good works, but now by the presence of his spirit you are given further ability to know his word. If you have allowed the spirit of God to live in you, he gives you the ability to increase in the knowledge of him through his word. Your ability to have wisdom and revelation in the knowledge of God and the things of God increase your better understanding of him. Now the true spiritual meanings of scriptures in the Bible come alive to you and with real understanding and context. The Bible becomes the source of your truth if the words in it make sense and directly appeal to you. When you have reached this stage then the Bible can work for you. You begin to believe those words, and what they can do for you becomes real. Now this is very interesting; the desires of your heart can be granted to you if you believe those words in the Bible about what you want done by God. For example, if you are flipping through the Bible and one of its verses talking about the healing of sick catches your eyes, when you are sick and you begin to believe that what that verse says can happen to you, then you can easily be healed. Additionally, as well, it may also be a verse talking about a healing which occurred to someone else and you believe that verse on healing, then the same miracle can happen to you. There is no reason whatever that what God has done in the past, cannot be done again.

What are the desires of our hearts? We must be careful not to believe that it is our natural material things God is talking about here. If you want to be a better student of the Bible, then you must first learn to look at the spiritual context of

Bible verses first before their physical context. In the above verse you will be tempted to believe that God is talking about worldly riches, honours, blessings, power, money, relationships, and all forms of pleasures. Yes, indeed there is merit in having and longing for these things, but to God they are all bonuses that you get when you have done his "will." Everything that is within God's "will," is spiritual. What will be the "will," of God that you don't desire to have, yet God desires that you should have it? Let us give examples of the things of the Spirit that we don't desire, yet they are critical for our life here on Earth. Things such as love, peace, joy, wisdom, knowledge and understanding plus much more. You can have all riches but when you lack peace, you cannot enjoy your riches. You can be married, but when there is a lack of love in that marriage, you cannot enjoy it. So, you can see with these few examples why spiritual things are more important than the physical things. God sees things differently than we do. Before you can rush to being a gospel preacher, he must first build in you the important characteristics such, patience, endurance and perseverance before he can allow you to preach and to have riches, in order not to be easily destroyed by them. Seeking after the spiritual things first before the physical things is better for us. Spiritual things are lovely and more durable than the physical things. May the desires of your heart be spiritual things over physical things every now and again.

John 15:16 You did not choose Me, but I chose you and appointed you that you should go and bear fruit, and that your fruit should remain, that whatever you ask the Father in My name He may give you. NKJV.

This verse has even taken these things up to the next level.

If God had chosen you before you had no knowledge of your calling, what about now that you have the knowledge of your calling? He can now easily let you know your assignment. God's assignment is not just about preaching the Bible, but what are you also gifted at? What can you do best beyond and above everyone else? That is your gift. For example, there are nine gifts of the Holy Spirit, therefore those who believe, you may be given the gift due to your measure of faith and capability. You cannot be gifted in all of them, but you can be gifted in a few of them based on your calling. For example, you can be gifted in speaking of tongues and not interpretation of it or you can be gifted in revelations of Bible verses but not in miracle performance of them. But the good news is that God can still give you what you desire to have out of the nine gifts. Above all, you cannot be a preacher of the Bible without authority and power to cast out demons. You cannot bear fruit in God's Kingdom without these two. Without these two gifts you will just be another preacher that the demons are not mindful and afraid of. In fact, the demons would love such preachers who are not productive to the kingdom of God.

When you are chosen by God then he will make sure that you will be fruitful. St Paul was called as an apostle and Jeremiah was called as a prophet and they were both fruitful in their own assignments. In fact, there is no reason why you cannot be successful in your assignment today. These two plus others were given their assignments by God himself and it was very difficult for them not to be fruitful. If you want your fruit to remain then you must focus on the hope of your calling. What does God want you to do? He will tell you it might be teaching or prophesying to the nations. Can you also be author of books,

CDs, sermons, Christian television network presenter, principal of a Christian school or a church administrator or minister? What can you do the best for your fruit to remain? Once you have found the hope of your calling it will be very difficult for you not to succeed because God will be with you. Your success is God's success, and he must do it for you to succeed.

WE AS CHRISTIANS ARE TO BE IN CHRIST AS THE SOURCE OF OUR SALVATION

There is nothing that is more important than the work of salvation no matter what we do for ourselves and for God on Earth. There is nothing that is more precious than the gift of salvation to us, in order to go and live with God in heaven. There is nothing we could pay, no matter how rich we may be with the material things of this world. Salvation is a gift of God to humanity. Although it is a gift offered by God to us, we must be willing and ready to receive it. It is a gift of God, yet it must be received by them who are willing to have it. Since Christ came to the world the door of salvation remains open for people from every tribe, community, society, and nation of Earth to come in before the door is suddenly closed. The door of salvation will not remain open forever as there is a time set for it. And that time is our lord Jesus Christ's second return to the Earth. Before Christ's return the door of salvation will be first closed and then comes Christ in the clouds to judge the dead and the living on Earth (revelation 1:7).

Although salvation is free to everyone, the requirement is that you must believe in Christ, and be baptised with both water and the Holy Spirit to have it. Those who will have this salvation after they are saved will continue to be obedient and willing to remain within God's "will" forever. Those who will have this salvation are the ones who are committed to the works and service of God's kingdom on Earth. Those who have accepted God's truth (the Bible) and who are committed to hearing God's voice can have the salvation. His voice can be heard through prayer, fasting, and reading the Bible in order to familiarise yourself with God's voice. When we do this then we cannot be caught or overtaken by that day because we have acquainted ourselves with the voice of the Holy Spirit.

WE MUST REMAIN IN CHRIST IF WE ARE TO GROW SPIRITUALLY

Walking with God is not an overnight thing, but it is rather an ongoing thing until he returns. In order to have better knowledge in things of God you need the training of the Holy Spirit who is in you. The spirit of God will take you from glory to glory when you are willing and obedient to his voice and instructions. The only reason we cannot grow in the things of God, is our unwillingness to practise hearing the voice and the instructions of the Holy Spirit. The way you cultivate this relationship is through daily prayer, fasting, reading the Bible, and listening to other great men and women, of God's account of building the relationship. God is willing that this relationship be established between you and him. The disappointment God has is that many people are not willing to establish this relationship with him, yet he wants to reach out to many people through those who are committed to hearing his voice and following his instructions. Imagine how many people can be healed in a day if we were readily available to be used by the Holy Spirit.

How do we establish this relationship? Well, we are spirit, and we must pay attention to what is happening within our spirit- person. As soon as we are born with the spirit of God, our spirit becomes activated with the things of God. What is being communicated to us comes from within us into our spirits from the spirit of God. We must learn to read the word of God and pray daily in order to establish this relationship. The word of God becomes the guiding star through which we can do all things. Before we can make important decisions of our lives, we must rush to God's word over the matter to see what God has to say about it.

Proverbs 4:20 My son, give attention to my words; Incline your ear to my sayings. 21 Do not let them depart from your eyes; Keep them in the midst of your heart; 22 For they are life to those who find them, And health to all their flesh. 23 Keep your heart with all diligence, for out of it spring the issues of life. NKJV.

If we want to grow, then we must pay attention to the words of God. We must believe it as the truth. We must apply that truth to our daily lives. The word must abide in us and us in the word. We must continue to practise the word of God until it comes alive to us, and use it over our situation. We must find time through our busy schedules to build on this relationship and maintain it continuously. When we do this there is nothing God cannot do through us, for us and others. God's word becomes the light to our path if we pay attention to it daily. We must also find time to have Bible study in groups at times because there may be some other people who may be better informed about Bible verses, than we are.

WE CAN ONLY BE PRODUCTIVE IN WHAT WE DO IF WE REMAIN IN CHRIST

There must be something that you are dominant in. Musicians dominate the music industry because they compose and sing songs, entrepreneurs dominate the market because they have ideas to run successful businesses, lawyers dominate courts because they have ability to study and interpret laws, preachers preach the word of God because they can understand Bible verses, and the list goes on. Something that people around you will miss if you were to be absent from them, is your gift from God. What you can do best, that is your gift from God. The main problem today with many people is that they chase after other people's gifts and successes. Just because someone else has success in that area does not mean that you are going to succeed in that area as well. The fact that so many people have succeeded in that area does not mean that everyone else will succeed in that area as well. We are all gifted, but differently. My gift may not be your gift and so the chances of your success by chasing after my gift may be minimal. Instead of chasing after other people's gifts, we must chase after the giver of gifts, who is God himself. God is the only deity that can give gifts to men and women who seek after them. The only way your fruits can remain in the Kingdom of God is to seek your gift in the Kingdom of God. Many people can easily discover their gifts, but many countless others may find it very difficult to find their gifts and they need mentors to help them discover their gifts within themselves. The only way we can be productive in this life is to find out what we can do the best in this life. That may be the "will" of God for our lives.

This is the question you must ask yourself as a Christian; What is the "will of God," for my life? What is that one thing which can please God to give to me, that is within his will? Not what I want from him for my life but what he wants me to have for my life. This one thing must be a thing from Heaven not from Earth. Child of God, there are things of Heaven and things of Earth. Obviously, the things of Heaven are better than the things of Earth because they are spiritual in nature, and permanent. We are invited to ask and to focus our attention to the better things of Heaven because of their spirituality and their durability.

We as Christians have been invited to ask for the things of Heaven, because we have been crucified and risen with Christ, giving us permission to seek after those things above. You must be excited by this. The things above are, amongst others, long life, knowledge, wisdom, understanding, power, counsel, and fear of God. Those with a good number of these things will succeed in life here on Earth and will overcome the challenges of this life. You must be excited by now to seriously seek after those things.

The things mentioned above can only be given to people if they believe in Jesus Christ as their personal saviour. These are things of God given to Christ to give to us. Those things are far better than the important things of Earth like, gold, silver, bronze, oil, and much more. Those things of Earth are not permanent, for they can change hands or forms many times. We must not crave for them because they are perishing.

Seek the things that are spiritual and have a permanent nature. They are things of God and God is readily waiting to give them to his children who please him. They are within his will for his children. Seek after the will of God for your life and you will never be disappointed and ashamed.

1 Kings 3:10-14 The speech pleased the Lord, that Solomon had asked this thing. Then God said to him: "Because you have asked this thing, and have not asked long life for yourself, nor have asked riches for yourself, nor have asked the life of your enemies, but have asked for yourself understanding to discern justice, behold, I have done according to your words; see, I have given you a wise and understanding heart, so that there has not been anyone like you before you, nor shall any like you arise after you. And I have also given you what you have not asked: both riches and honour, so that there shall not be anyone like you among the kings all your days. So if you walk in My ways, to keep My statutes and My commandments, as your father David walked, then I will lengthen your days." NKJV.

AS BORN-AGAIN CHRISTIANS WE MUST ASK GOD FOR WHAT WE WANT IN JESUS NAME

YOUR PROVISION IS IN CHRIST

Provision means God is the provider of all things that you and I need. Whether it is food, shelter, clothes, health, favour, victory, security, peace, love or joy. The main reason why many people have missed and will continue to miss salvation is the fact that they are busy providing for themselves and their families and they have no time for God. This has become an excuse of many people and the reason why they do not have time to serve and worship God. It is even difficult for such people who have amassed for themselves the wealth of this world, to have time, energy, and resources to give to the services and worship of God. Most people think that when they are rich every aspect of their life is secured and protected, yet this is not true. I don't really know whether it is the devil or our ignorance that has made us not believe God's truth about our provision, yet it is abundantly stated in the Bible. If God has already provided the things that we have no ability to provide for ourselves such as air, sun, moon and stars, why then can't he provide for us the things we think we can provide for ourselves. If he has provided freely to everyone, then why do we still doubt he can channel things to us individually. For example, we have air individually and sun individually just to name two things. This begs the question, which is better to have, the provider of things, or things? The answer to this choice is yours. I am just highlighting all options for you, to make abundantly clear to you the better choice you can take. You can choose to go after these things alone, but rest assured you will be hindered by your enemy the devil. This is because the devil wants to give the resources of God to his children who have made covenant with him. This is one of the reasons God wants you to get his resources through him, in Christ, in order to be protected, and for that matter also to avoid the resistance and the hindrances of the devil.

Matthew 6:33 But seek first the kingdom of God and His righteousness, and all these things shall be added to you. NKJV.

The above verse is a clear indication and invitation by God to us for our provision by God. Think about this; he is the creator of all things, and he is inviting you to have provision of all things. This must blow-your mind. You work hard by yourself to provide for your family, yet God is inviting you not to work hard and provide for your family. But there are strings attached to these provisions which is the statement seek "first his kingdom and his righteousness," to obtain them. God is telling you out of the above statement; give me your time and the energy you are using to work for yourself, to worship me, and I will provide for your family. That is what he is saying to you today. There are important things about the kingdom of God that humans have no ability to obtain unless they believe in God. For example, long life, salvation, peace, love, joy among others. These things cannot be obtained by people's hard work; they must first believe in the kingdom of God. To me these are the necessities of life, yet we brush them aside as if we are masters of them. The ability to have long life on Earth is never determined by the individual and so is the salvation of souls to go and live in heaven with God, after death. So, it will be now wiser for you to seek first the kingdom of heaven before the material resources of this world. God's wisdom is always wiser than ours, and there are always better reasons as to why he asks us first to do certain things in a certain way, before he can bless us with the things we want.

As stated above God has a provision for every single person born on Earth. He has the budget for the seven billion people who occupy this planet. It is also his desire for us to live long on Earth to enjoy his provisions for us. The world has enough resources for us all. But why are these resources always not enough for us all? Here comes the answer to this question. We live in a world of men and women who have the fallen nature that causes economic mismatch of the abundant resources. Many men and women who happen to have an opportunity to control and distribute resources, turn to domination, and manipulate the resources to their advantage over others. The idea that things will never be enough for all of us is deeply rooted in the fallen nature of mankind. The idea that things will never be enough for us all cause men and women to be corrupt and greedy for the control of these material resources. Hoarding of material resources is a sin. These actions by a few people have made some get resources easily, while others get them at great expense of their time and energy, and others never get them at all. There is a constant struggle today on Earth for God's resources between rich and poor, employers and employees, parents and their children, tenants and landlords, politicians and activists and the list go on. If there is only one word, I can use to describe this battle, it would be "**manipulation**," of resources. The analogy always given by those who have power over the distribution of resources is that the resources will not be enough for us all. This is calculated in their minds because they have no understanding of the living God, who is infinite in knowledge and with infinite resources. When we limit God in our thinking then we will always lack things including material things. We will continue to scramble as nations, people and communities over what he has already provided and forget what he will provide next. For example, the God who fed the five thousand people with two fish and five loaves of bread was unimaginable in the eyes of his disciples before the miracle took place. They gave many reasons as to why the two fish and five loaves of bread would not be enough. This is exactly what happens to us today. We create many reasons in our minds why resources will not be enough for us all and we may end up in shortage. When we reject God relying on only the reasoning and logic in our minds, we end up in lack. Let's now investigate further why men and women think this way.

The concept of lack is ingrained in people's minds. People who are poor think they will be poor forever and people who are rich think their riches will never end, or that they want more to protect themselves from future poverty. Why is this? Because of the fallen nature of mankind. The rebellion of Adam and Eve, and thus all of humanity in the garden of Eden came with the dangerous consequences of a curse. As the result of the rebellion, the land was cursed, and the ability of the land to produce sufficient for mankind was reduced and humans had to work harder to produce from the land. Humanity was also cursed because of the disobedience. You see how isolation from God can be deadly. Isolation from God also means isolation from our source of blessings and provisions. Whether it is our own fault or the fault of others we will always lack as humanity. We have today many factors of production such as land, money, labour, and ideas, yet we are still poor. Some have used production methods well, yet they are still poor, or they can be dragged back into poverty because of other people's discrimination, drug abuse, wars, ill health, jealousy, hatred, lack of education, and government taxation, rules, and regulations. Furthermore, government elites across nations have concentrated and amassed for themselves treasures of the nation's leaving a lot of families, communities, and societies in poverty. We are nothing without God. No man or woman can stop humanity's greed apart from God.

Having said that we must also be careful not to categorise poverty today as a result of sin, because God has corrected the curse through his son Jesus Christ. All sin, iniquity and transgression has been removed by the death of our lord Jesus Christ on the cross. But why are we still poor, particularly those in the community? God himself admits that there will always be poor among us. But why is this admission for the Lord? Let us investigate.

John 12:8 *For the poor you have with you always, but Me you do not have always."* (NKJV).

This verse has given us the answer. Firstly, some of us will always be poor because we have rejected God from being part of our lives. For example, there are communities, societies, and nations in the world today where it is an offense to teach or to mention the name of our lord Jesus Christ. Examples are China, some parts of India and almost all the Muslim nations. Secondly, some of us believe in God and still are ignorant of his ways and his laws of wealth and riches. A good example, in this case are some African nations where most people still worship their traditional gods, and this has increased ignorance within them. It is an offence to God to worship gods fashioned from what he created. The world is interlinked and poverty in one part of the world affects other parts of the world. Because of the lack of knowledge about God in some of these nations, the leaders have gained wealth through exploitation, force, corruption, greed and thuggery, putting a lot of people into poverty. Thirdly, there will always be people among us in society who will not have the ability to provide for themselves, for example the disabled, sick, orphans, foreigners, and widows. We have the responsibility as people of nations and governments of nations to look after them if God has blessed us with resources or put us in the position to distribute resources. There is a punishment associated with not looking after these categories of people (Mathew 25:44-46).

Even though God has provided the solution to the problems

of the world, people of the world continue to suffer today from their rejection of God. Just as Adam discovered, when we reject God, we are cursed and punished. As a result of this rejection of God, humanity continues to experience natural disasters which destroy communities and sometimes effect whole nations. This in turn means that the livelihoods of people, and their means of earning are jeopardised, resulting in more poverty.

People may also lack through their own making. People who have acquired riches because they have gone to the devil to seek after his riches will always experience demonic destruction. If you have participated in human sacrifice then nothing will stop, you from experiencing demonic attacks because the blood of that human being is on your head. There is no free blood whether it is yours or that of your loved ones to be shed without a cause. The devil will give you temporary riches, but it comes with enormous consequences of death and lack in the future. When you worship the devil, you have declared yourself as the enemy of God. God is the creator of all things including the riches you have gotten from the devil.

In contrast to this, those who have experienced the blessings of God must also share their wealth with the poor. We have the responsibility to share with those who lack if we are to continue to receive from God. The reason we are blessed is to be a blessing to those who lack for some reasons known only to them. We must be careful with the temptation that comes with acquisition and the distribution of wealth. Things such as pride and arrogance, self-sufficiency, complacency, loss of focus, lust, dissatisfaction, and more importantly, divided attention on God. There is nothing that we are blessed with and for, that will buy the salvation of our souls from God. God will always have more for us no matter what we have or do not have in this life. That is why we must not lose focus on him. He is our great father, and he deserves to be worshipped and served by us all, all the time.

We must always depend on God as our source for all our needs and wants. Whether poor or rich we need God's provision, protection and his spirit in order to worship him. A rich person needs God's salvation, and a poor person needs God's provision and salvation. We are reminded on many occasions in the Bible that we must be mindful of our riches in order not to deny God and miss our salvation and about our poverty not to steal in order to miss our salvation (Proverbs 30:9). There are enough provisions in God's kingdom for everyone. God proved himself in this, many times, when he fed the entire Hebrew people in the wilderness with manna and quails. Those who gathered what they needed lacked nothing, and those who gathered more than they needed found that by the next morning, their excess was ruined. Every time we come to God, none of us shall lack. All we need is to change our mind-set and have right attitudes about God, and we will never lack his provisions. It is God who successfully fought off the corruption in the nation of Israel and it is God who can fight off the rampant corruption we see in many nations today. When this happens, there will be enough resources for all of us.

Let me tell you this, you must give God the first in your life, before he can give back to you. He loves it when you first give to him. For example, whether it is the Samaritan woman at the well or whether it is the widow of Zarephath or whether it is his disciple, he had to ask them first to provide for him, for him to perform the miracle in their situations. God does it to test our hearts whether we are willing to give to him before he can give to us. God's giving to us will always be in abundance and that is why he needs to develop right attitudes within us, by inviting us first to give to him. If we cannot give to God and other people, than why will God give to us? God also does it to discourage idleness. There is nothing God hates like idleness. In fact, the first responsibility God gave Adam in the garden of Eden was not his family but his work. Apostle Paul is very clear on this; "if anyone is not willing to work then they should not eat (2 Thessalonians 3:10)." It is that simple. God created us to work for him and for ourselves.

Finally, we must give to God what belongs to God and that is our souls and spirits. There is nothing God delights himself in more than the broken spirits that come to him. He desires the gifts of broken souls and spirits more than our own other sacrifices to him. The primary reasons among others why God created mankind was for worship, praise and singing. He loves it when his children come to him in worship.

Matthew 22:21 They said to Him, "Caesar's." And He said to them, "Render therefore to Caesar the things that are Caesar's, and to God the things that are God's." NKJV.

The above verse can be interpreted this way; give God your spirit because he is the creator of your spirit and give Caesar the money because he is the creator of the money. God hates it when we go and bow down to idols and powerful world leaders. By doing this you are lowering yourself before his other creations of which you are part. God wants you to worship him alone and no other parts of his creation. When our souls and spirits are right with God, then nothing will stop our blessings. We must learn to give to God before he can give back to us. He is just looking for what we have that he can bless.

YOUR PROTECTION IS IN CHRIST

The living God is the battle himself. He does not want us to go to war ourselves but rather he wants to go to war on our behalf. The children of God whose hearts are troubled with many worries of this life are protected by God. God is in control of what your hearts are troubled about. Think about it, there is nothing God cannot do. Our Lord Jesus comforted his disciples who were troubled about his upcoming death, and other pressing needs. In the same way he teaches us to trust him about the things that often cause us to worry. He wants us to know that he is in charge. Think about how many disasters you survived, which surpassed your expectations to make it through them? God is the same yesterday, today and tomorrow, meaning he oversees your life. He created all things, and he oversees all things, meaning that there is nothing he cannot do for you.

All you need is to have trust and faith in him and his son Jesus Christ and everything will be alright for you. Faith means it is the only way you can have what you want from God. Trust means that God will come to your aid no matter what. Relax and spend a lot of your time in prayer and worship instead of complaining about everything. There is nothing that can defeat God. He will come for you when your time is right. You must be appreciative of the little he is doing in your life. He is building you up for better faith, character, and discipline, so that when his blessings come, they may not destroy you. Maturity matters in everything. Knowledge matters in everything, particularly the knowledge of God. You must be rather patient in training instead of getting the blessings that will destroy you once received.

God knows you better than you think. He knows everything about you. He created you with your blessings in mind. Now that you have returned to him, everything about you will be given back to you. If there is one thing you must be appreciative to God about, then it is your salvation. Have hope because everything is going to be alright. Keep fighting the good fight of faith. The ability to fight is already within you.

James 4:7 Submit yourselves, then, to God. Resist the devil, and he will flee from you. NKJV.

The only way you can defeat Satan who is tempting you is through your submission to God. We must submit to God in our thoughts, words, and actions. We must be willing and obedient to what God wants to achieve through us. We may have many plans, but it is only the will of God that will prevail in our lives. Instead of wasting time on our own desires we must seek first the will of God in what we are going through, whether it is what we brought on ourselves, or God allowed for us. When we submit to God's righteousness, truth, and justice through prayer and fasting, we can more easily identify God's will in the situation we are facing. When we are under attack, we can go to God, through prayer very quickly, to discern what we need to do in the situation we are facing.

Now it can be easy to resist the devil when you have the knowledge of God. Knowledge of God in everything matters if you are to win against Satan every time you are under attack. This is what many people do not know. When you become a Christian, you have declared rebellion against Satan who is the ruler of the world. We must not be ignorant of this fact. Because the power Satan has cannot be matched with our power. God has given us the authority of the Earth, but he has withheld from us the power for his children to defeat Satan. If we had power, God would have not come to die on our behalf to defeat Satan who had power of death over mankind. When we have successfully submitted ourselves to God, God releases power to us to resist and defeat Satan. For example, the weapons such as the word, faith, truth, righteousness, grace, peace. joy, love, mercy, compassion, fasting and prayer and the blood of our lord Jesus Christ, can be given to us in abundance to defeat Satan. When you have these weapons at your disposal there is no reason Satan cannot flee from you.

All storms in your life are for God to fix. God is faithful he will never allow you to be tempted beyond what you are able. The way has already been provided out of your storm. Stop complaining about it and let God take control of it. If any situation in your life is too big and challenging to solve, then it belongs to God to solve. Think about it, there is no storm God can't fix. Whether it is a storm of unemployment, promotion, succession plan, divorce, rebellious children, abuse, neglect, wars, floods, fires, violence, fear, doubt, and the list go on and on. God is in control no matter what you think about your situation. If God had not prepared a way out of your storm, he wouldn't have allowed it. He has already made a way out for you. While you are experiencing turbulence and the darkest storm in your life, unsure of the way out, stay calm and let the Lord take control of it.

1 Corinthians 10:13 No temptation has overtaken you except such as is common to man; but God is faithful, who will not allow you to be tempted beyond what you are able, but with the temptation will also make the way of escape, that you may be able to bear it. NKJV.

St Paul has concluded this decisively in the book of Romans 8:31-39. In these verses we are told that there will be always problems in the world, but they are all put under the believers' feet. These problems, no matter how they may show up in our lives must know that they have all been defeated by Christ on our behalf. You see what defeats us in every situation is not the problem itself but our mindset in the situation. If we think the problems are too much for us, we are most likely to be defeated by the problems. But if we believe no matter how big or small the problems are, we will defeat them, then we are most likely to be victorious over them. For example, if the soldier goes to war thinking that he is going to be killed during the war, then he will be killed. In any war, whether physical or spiritual, what you think before, in and after the battle matters if you are going to win. What does this tell you? The condition of our mind determines our victory. Well, we are given a condition of our mindset here, if we are to win every battle in this life. We must always think as victors, and we will always be victors.

Romans 8:31-39 What then shall we say to these things? If God is for us, who can be against us? He who did not spare His own Son, but delivered Him up for us all, how shall He not with Him also freely give us all things? Who shall bring a charge against God's elect? It is God who justifies. Who is he who condemns? It is Christ who died, and furthermore is also risen, who is even at the right hand of God, who also makes intercession for us. Who shall separate us from the love of Christ? Shall tribulation, or distress, or persecution, or famine, or nakedness, or peril, or sword? As it is written: "For Your sake we are killed all day long; We are accounted as sheep for the slaughter." Yet in all these things we are more than conquerors through Him who loved us. For I am persuaded that neither death nor life, nor angels nor principalities nor powers, nor things present nor things to come, nor height nor depth, nor any other created thing, shall be able to separate us from the love of God which is in Christ Jesus our Lord. NKJV.

I personally like these words "persuasion" and "persuaded". "Persuasion" means, set of beliefs whereas "persuaded" means doing something because you have been convinced by truth to do it. Let's talk about the grammar a little bit; persuasion is a noun and persuaded is a verb. Let's bring the subject which is the noun "persuasion" and the verb "persuaded" and put them in agreement. This is called subject and verb agreement. Have you ever heard of this saying, what you think is who you are or for that matter who you become? This saying simply means that what you believe is you and that is what you must act on it. Let go back to our two words persuasion and persuaded. What you think is from you is from your mind and what you do comes from what you believe. So, when you are persuaded, you are going to do what you believe is the truth in your mind. St. Paul is telling us that what we do matters, and it must come from what we believe in our mind, and if we think this way, we can never be defeated by challenges of this life such as death, life, angels, principalities, powers, things present or things to come, height or depth, or any other created thing. He is telling us that these things will always challenge us but because of God's love for us through Jesus Christ, who has defeated all these things, we cannot be separated from him by these things. This is your victory right here; you should take it and celebrate it.

He even goes on further to say that what we have is not just a simple victory but conquering. When you are a conqueror, you can take back territories over which you had no power before.

You will now dominate everything that comes your way in the future. For example, if you have been diagnosed with a deadly disease such as cancer and you use the word of God to defeat it, then there are no future cancers that come your way that you will never defeat. Not cancer alone but other future disease that may come your way. In addition to that when you have learned how to defeat cancer then you can even go ahead and teach cancer patients ways to defeat their cancers. So, you have become a conqueror, conquering diseases by setting people free from their sickness using the word of God.

YOUR WORSHIP OF GOD MUST BE IN CHRIST

What caused the battle between God and Satan was the worship in heaven. The battle in heaven was the battle about who was to be worshipped - God or Satan. This battle is still ongoing today in the world. This battle is over your soul as a human being, over worship. God demands worship and Satan demands worship from you, whether you like it or not. There are only two spiritual kingdoms on Earth, the kingdom of God and the kingdom of Satan. That is why people who accept God worshipped God, and those people who reject God end up worshipping Satan anyway, whether knowingly or unknowingly. God uses legitimate authority to require his children to worship him whereas Satan uses illegitimate authority for his children to worship him. God demands his children to be holy and obedient to worship him, whereas Satan demands his children to be unholy and disobedient to worship him. For people to worship God, they must be free from sin, whereas when people want to worship Satan, they must be sinful.

The only way Satan can get people to worship him is to get them to sin so that God can disown them. Satan uses magicians, sorcerers, witches, spiritists and mediums to intimidate, manipulate, and dominate people. Satan seems to entrap many people because of corrupt human nature that has the propensity to sin. Satan easily can stir up the desires of the flesh within human beings to commit sin. When the desire of mankind become too obsessive and demanding, people are most likely to commit sin. When one desires something so badly and there is an opportunity to get it then he or she can easily commit sin. That is why the desire of money becomes an issue above all else. If men and women have uncontrollable desires to be rich, they are most likely going to use any means to get rich. Satan can easily give people riches in return for their worship. People want quick riches and Satan has no problem giving riches to those who have made it the desire of their souls. That is why people can easily trade-off their souls for riches with Satan. This is a complete deception by Satan because he knows very well that this world is passing away with its riches and those who love riches will go and spend the rest of their eternity in hell because of their desires. We must resist the devil's riches because they are not as valuable as our souls and spirits. He tempted Jesus Christ with riches of this world but Jesus Christ resisted him and so we should also resist him. Satan was so desperate for Jesus Christ to worship him because he knew that had Jesus Christ given in to his deception, there would have been no salvation for mankind.

Matthew 4: 8 Again, the devil took Him up on an exceedingly high mountain and showed Him all the kingdoms of the world and their glory. 9 And he said to Him, "All these things I will give

You if You will fall down and worship me." 10 Then Jesus said to him, "Away with you, Satan! For it is written, 'You shall worship the Lord your God, and Him only you shall serve." NKJV.

Put God above all else; if you are poor, you will need God for provision, protection, and worship and if you are rich, you will need God for provision, protection, and worship. Whether we are rich or poor we are not any better before God. Never trust in your wealth, riches, and money as they can change hands many times. And above all else all of us need his salvation for our souls which cannot be bought at any cost. This is the message we preach. This is the message God has entrusted us with. Why am I putting this clearly at the onset? The biggest threat to people's salvation is their riches. It is more likely for a rich person not to be saved than a poor person. It is even harder for a rich person to find time and energy to serve and to worship God. The Bible is very clear that you cannot serve two masters - God and riches. It is impossible because you will give one your full attention, time, and energy over the other. If you choose the riches of this world, then you are most likely going to miss out on God's salvation. If you choose God over the riches of this world, then you are most likely going to miss out on the riches of this world.

God's kingdom economy: there is no money in heaven. The only thing that can go to heaven is your spirit and soul. God is more interested in building your character than your money. When men and women preach to you, let them preach to you a lot about you changing your character over you giving them money. God's kingdom economy is not based on money. God created mankind who created the money. When God is pleased with men and women, he does not reward them with money but with knowledge, wisdom and understanding to help them create money. God is more interested in your character than your money. The only treasure you can store in heaven is your body, soul, and spirit.

Worship is a gift. The best gift you can give to God is your spirit. He loves it the most when his children come to him in their bodies, souls, and spirits to worship him. He created our spirits and loves it if we return to him in worship. The best gift God gives back to you in return for your worship, is his spirit (Holy Spirit). Service is a gift. Your service to God and others is a very important gift to God. Your gift can range from material resources, human resources, and other forms of services.

2

THE HOLY SPIRIT IN YOU

The Holy Spirit is the kingdom of heaven's representative on Earth. He has been permanently assigned to us by God until the end of all things. It is important to note that the Holy Spirit is a person, but a Spirit person. The Bible speaks to us that he can be grieved and quenched (Ephesians 4:30, 1 Thessalonians 5:19). But not only that, he is a teacher, reminder, helper, advocate, and a guide for our future among other things. Because he is a spiritual being, you cannot see him, but he can see you. He is the third person of the trinity; God the father, God the son and God the Holy Spirit. How did the world receive the Holy Spirit? We know that God was here on Earth in the person of our Lord Jesus Christ. When he left the Earth, he promised to go and send us the Holy Spirit, fifty days after his departure. Christ instructed the disciples to wait in Jerusalem until they had received the Holy Spirit. Fifty days later after his departure from the Earth, the arrival of the Holy Spirit on the day of Pentecost was marked by visible signs such as divided tongues, fire and mighty rushing wind resting on each one of the disciples (Acts 2:4). For the first time in the history of humanity the biggest miracle occurred as disciples of different backgrounds spoke in different languages, yet they understood each other. This became a turning point in the relationship between God and humanity, as for the first time God was able to officially communicate with mankind through mankind.

Why did God send to us the Holy Spirit?

We can never know things of God without God teaching them to us. God is in heaven, and we are on Earth. God is a spirit, and we are spirits in bodies confined to the Earth. We were created to be the permanent residents of the Earth, in charge of the Earth, to look after all God's creations on Earth. Because we are not the creators of the things on Earth, we need help and that is why the Spirit of God was sent to us. The Spirit of God was sent to us to help in the understanding of things of God on Earth. His roles among other things are to help, to teach and to guide us to all truth about God's creations.

Christ made a profound statement about the Holy Spirit: *John 14:16,17 "And I will pray the Father, and He will give you another helper, that He may abide with you forever, the Spirit of truth, whom the world cannot receive, because it neither sees Him nor knows Him; but you know Him, for He dwells with you and will be in you."* NKJV.

In these two verses, it is crystal clear that the people of the world can never see nor know the Holy Spirit. Why is this? Because they cannot receive him. Why can they not receive him? Because they must be born again by the Holy Spirit. Unless you are born of the Spirit of God you cannot know the things of God. But not only does he dwell in those people who are born-again. Those who have allowed their bodies to be used by God. Those who are born of water and the Spirit. The baptism of water is the baptism for the remission of sins, and the baptism of the Holy Spirit is the baptism to allow the Spirit of God to live in you. He can never live in a person who has not confessed their sins. He hates sins because that was what had separated him from Adam and Eve.

THE HOLY SPIRIT AS OUR TEACHER

No one knows the things of God unless they are taught by God. Just as no one knows the things of the world and particularly things of men unless they are taught by men. We have our pastors, parents and teachers who teach us things about humanity. The same rule applies to the things of God; no one can teach us things of God unless by the Spirit of God. Teaching is one of the important roles of the Holy Spirit and it is why he was sent to us. Whether they are pastors on the pulpits, in the churches or individual believers in the community, no one can claim to know the things of God unless they have been taught by the Holy Spirit. If someone is teaching the things of God without acknowledging the Holy Spirit as a teacher through him, then they are teaching wrong things. The Bible is very clear about the Holy Spirit being the teacher of all things of God.

John 14:26 But the Advocate, the Holy Spirit, whom the Father will send in my name, will teach you all things and will remind you of everything I have said to you. NKJV.

This verse is loaded with a lot of information that needs separate explanations but let us leave the rest for next time and focus on the teaching and remembrance. We know in the world when we are taught, we are taught by those human professionals who are well trained and equipped with knowledge in the subjects they teach. We cannot be teachers in the world without being trained. If we are teachers, then we must be knowledgeable above those that we teach. The teachers are just as knowledgeable and intelligent according to the information and the data they have on the subjects. The information and data the teachers use to teach their students, they received from other well-trained professionals. The data and information in those books and curricula are determined by the governments' educational bodies and experts in the subject. In the human context, it is not an easy thing to be a teacher, as there are requirements needed for one to qualify. But not only that, it is an inherent part of human nature to forget things quickly. If a teacher does not constantly update his or her knowledge, skills, and experiences, they may easily forget.

The same thing applies, when it comes to the teaching of things of God, particularly teaching the Bible. No one can understand the Bible more than its author, the Holy Spirit. It is not only the Bible teaching that requires the Holy Spirit teaching but the whole creation on Earth and heaven. The Bible is a template explaining how things on Earth and heaven were created by God. No matter how human beings try to understand the whole creation of God, they cannot because they are not its creators. It will just be like buying a car and trying to use it without the manufacturer's manual and the instructor teaching you everything about the car. Whether it is the Bible or the things in the natural environment we need God to teach them to us.

Let us come back to the teaching of the Bible because it is

critical to be well understood as it contains everything God has created. The Bible is a word of God and it was written by those inspired by the Holy Spirit. Those who wrote the Bible had specific instructions, visions, dreams, voices, prophecies, signs, and wonders from the Holy Spirit.

Acts:2 ¹⁷ ‹And it shall come to pass in the last days, says God, That I will pour out of My Spirit on all flesh; Your sons and your daughters shall prophesy, Your young men shall see visions, Your old men shall dream dreams. ¹⁸ And on My menservants and on My maidservants, I will pour out My Spirit in those days; And they shall prophesy. ¹⁹ I will show wonders in heaven above and signs in the Earth beneath: Blood and fire and vapor of smoke. ²⁰ The sun shall be turned into darkness, And the moon into blood, Before the coming of the great and awesome day of the Lord. ²¹ And it shall come to pass That whoever calls on the name of the Lord Shall be saved.› NKJV.

We cannot surely know the truth about God and his creation unless we are taught by God himself. No matter the human teachers we may have, they will not give us a correct and exact full understanding of the Bible. Not even those who are Bible linguists understand everything about it. We must be willing to be taught directly by the Holy Spirit, no matter who we are. Our Earthly knowledge is so limited on things of man let alone things of God, and for this reason we must allow the Spirit of God to lead and guide us into all truth. It is for this reason that every believer must be independent of all the human teachers. This does not mean that you cannot learn and hear from them, but they are not the final authority to teach you the truth about God and meaning of things. It is a good starting point to have human teachers but if you want to go deep in the things of God, then you must seek the teachings by the Holy Spirit.

THE HOLY SPIRIT CONVICTS US OF OUR SIN

The meaningful sermons that convict people of their sins come from the teaching of the Holy Spirit. It is only the spirit-led and spirit-filled preacher that can preach a sermon that is soul-touching for people to repent of their sins and turn to God. The way we perceive the word of God enables us to change our sinful character, conduct, word, emotions, and thoughts. The word of God becomes a mirror in which we can see our good or bad conduct. It is not good enough to think that we are good by our own standards of judgement or the judgement of others. It is almost certain that there is nothing humans can do without selfish ambition or self-gratification. For example, we do things sometimes to claim credit or to be seen by others as good people. One of the reasons why many people reject God is the fact that they want to claim credit for what they do. As human beings, we focus a lot on the outer rather than the inside part of us in order to be seen by others as good people. There is nothing that mankind does without selfish acts, they have no knowledge and fear of the Lord. When we praise or are praised by others it is always an abomination to the lord. What man praises is not acceptable to the lord. We must always focus on God over man's approval. Sin is an integral part of human nature, and no one is immune from It. Sin is deeply embedded within us. It is within our human character. In addition to that our own desires and ambitions have the potential to get us to sin.

Unless we admit that we are sinners, God can do nothing for us. Sin is what separated mankind from God. Christ came to Earth purposely to die for our sins. We are sinful in nature, and no one knows this more than the God who created us. John the Apostle said unless we confess our sins, we deceive ourselves and the truth is not in us (1 John 1:8). It is either a truth within us or a lie within us. Our lord Jesus Christ said, it is not what goes into man that defiles the man but what comes out of man.

Matthew 15:17 "Don't you see that whatever enters the mouth goes into the stomach and then out of the body? [18] *But the things that come out of a person›s mouth come from the heart, and these defile them.* [19] *For out of the heart come evil thoughts; murder, adultery, sexual immorality, theft, false testimony, slander.* [20] *These are what defile a person; but eating with unwashed hands does not defile them.» NKJV.*

Sin is an embedded part of human nature, and no one can deny this fact. No single person can claim to have not sinned. And if they people claimed to have not sinned then they cannot claim to have no sinful nature. Unrepented sin leads to death and that is why God wants us to repent to be saved. The presence of God within us gives us true repentance. The more we get closer to God the more we will admit our sins. The Holy Spirit within us will expose every sinful nature within us.

THE HOLY SPIRIT LEADS US TO GODLY RIGHTEOUSNESS

Righteousness is defined as the quality of being morally true and just. Righteousness is a moral character of God. No human being is morally true and just apart from God. No human being is right in terms of character, conscience, conduct and command. By the standards of God's laws alone, no human being was able to attain God's righteousness and that is why

Christ had to come and die for us. The righteousness of God was obtained by Christ's obedience and willingness to die on the cross for our sins. No one knows better than the God who created us. He created us with a corrupt body of sin and death. In every single human being lies the law of sin and death in their body and we cannot obtain God's righteousness without his help. Therefore, righteousness is gift of God to those who believe in his son Jesus Christ.

Those who believe in God and his son Jesus Christ obtain their righteousness through the law of life. To obtain the righteousness of God, we who believe in Jesus Christ must live by the Holy Spirit. The Holy Spirit of God has nine gifts and nine fruits that he gives to the children of God. When we allow the Holy Spirit to live inside of us, we automatically obtain gifts and fruits. Without this, no one would obtain the righteousness of God.

Galatians 5:16 I say then: Walk in the Spirit, and you shall not fulfill the lust of the flesh. 17 For the flesh lusts against the Spirit, and the Spirit against the flesh; and these are contrary to one another, so that you do not do the things that you wish. 18 But if you are led by the Spirit, you are not under the law. 19 Now the works of the flesh are evident, which are: adultery, fornication, uncleanness, lewdness, 20 idolatry, sorcery, hatred, contentions, jealousies, outbursts of wrath, selfish ambitions, dissensions, heresies, 21 envy, murders, drunkenness, revelries, and the like; of which I tell you beforehand, just as I also told you in time past, that those who practice such things will not inherit the kingdom of God. 22 But the fruit of the Spirit is love, joy, peace, longsuffering, kindness, goodness, faithfulness, 23 gentleness, self-control. Against such there is no law. 24 And those who are Christ's have crucified the flesh with its passions and desires. 25 If we live in the Spirit, let us also walk in the Spirit. 26 Let us not become conceited, provoking one another, envying one another. NKJV.

The Holy Spirit will enable us to avoid God Judgement

Unfortunately, what many people don't know is that the ruler of this world – Satan has been judged. The verdict was rendered against Satan in heaven. Satan was found guilty of deception and destruction not only in heaven but also on Earth and has been sentenced to life imprisonment. Even as this verdict was executed in part because he was permanently expelled out of heaven, Satan continues to deceive many people today to go to hell with him.

John 16:8 And when He has come, He will convict the world of sin, and of righteousness, and of judgment: 9 of sin, because they do not believe in Me; 10 of righteousness, because I go to My Father and you see Me no more; 11 of judgment, because the ruler of this world is judged. NKJV.

It is the responsibility of the Holy Spirit to let the world know, especially those who continue to reject Jesus Christ and his work of salvation, that Satan is doomed, and siding with him will also mean doom for those who reject the work of salvation. He continues to deceive the people of Earth today through false teachers, false teachings, false doctrines, false miracles, false power, false riches, and false religions. He continues to exercise power over those who reject God and his son Jesus Christ.

Our Lord Jesus Christ dealt a final blow to Satan's dominance of the Earth when he died on the cross. He came purposely to the Earth to formally reconcile humanity back to God. What separated humanity from God is sin. Our sinful nature was crucified on the cross through Christ. God gave Christ a human body to defeat Satan who had power of death because of the sin in the flesh of mankind. What used to give Satan power over humanity was the law of sin and death which was pronounced by God against them. Today those who believe in Jesus Christ are set free from the law of sin and death and so Satan has no power to kill them. However, it is also important to note that those Christians who continue to live a sinful lifestyle, continue to give Satan power to kill them. The Holy Spirit has the responsibility to remind Christians of this fact if they want to go and live in heaven. Finally, if you continue to reject Christ to the point of death, then you will be judged by God for your own sins. This judgement of God is one of the reasons we preach to the world that they may be saved to avoid the wrath of God, which will be poured out on the unbelieving world. Christ will return not as a lamb of God, who takes away the sins of the world, but as king to judge the world of its sins and to reign on Earth with his children.

THE HOLY SPIRIT WILL LEAD US TO ALL TRUTH ABOUT GOD

The Holy Spirit is a spirit of truth. Christ is the truth. He will not only teach you about the truth but will also guide you to all truth. The Holy Spirit will teach you all things about Jesus Christ and he will also show you all the truth about him. Our Lord Jesus Christ, as it was prophesied, was conceived and born, and anointed to teach the word and heal the sick by the Holy Spirit. The work of the Holy Spirit is so critical to anyone who would want to know the truth about God's kingdom.

Whether it is the teaching of the Bible, doctrinal issues, or revelation of the deeper meaning of words in the bible, these are all dependent upon the Holy Spirit. It is the work of the Holy Spirit to expose the works of false teachers of the word. Human words are always different from the Holy Spirit's words. For example, the Holy Spirit will back up any prophecy, by making sure that it comes to fruition. The testimony of the words through the Holy Spirit and his servants is what the people rely on as truth. Deep things of God are revealed to us by the Holy Spirit. All the miracles and healings are conducted through the power of the Holy Spirit.

THE HOLY SPIRIT WILL BRING TO OUR REMEMBRANCE THE THINGS OF THE PAST

The past is what we have lived. Past is where we have seen the former moves and experiences of God in our lives. Past is where we have assurances of God's encounters with us, and we can move forward with this confidence in us. For example, the former moves of God in our lives would have been in the forms of voice conversations, visions, dreams, prophecies, or any other miraculous encounters with the living God. All of these become the basis of our belief that God exists.

But there is a problem connected with the past, which is human forgetfulness. It is inherent within human nature that we forget quickly. It is for this reason that the Holy Spirit was assigned to us to bring to remembrance those encounters of the past with the living God. The Holy Spirit is a spiritual being who does not forget because he is God. But not only that, every encounter we had in the past was through him. That is why our Lord Jesus Christ promised to go and send him to us. All the doctrinal teachings and prophecies, miracles, signs, and wonders Christ taught us had to be brought to our remembrance by the Holy Spirit. For example, I had an encounter with him when I was ten years old, way back in 1988. In that encounter with him, he asked me this question; What will your life be after this life? Because I was very young, I had no knowledge of him, and over years I struggled answering the question until recently when he manifested himself to me in a dream. After many encounters now with the Holy Spirit, I was reminded that it was he who had asked me that question in the past.

THE HOLY SPIRIT AS A GUIDE ON OUR DAILY PRESENT ACTIVITIES

The Spirit of God is our friend. He is willing to commune with us daily on our individual matters including studying the Bible, prayer, fasting and preaching the gospel. The word of God comes alive with the revelation of its verses and their true meaning by the Holy Spirit. The Holy Spirit reveals to the believer the deep things of God, things no man or woman knows or is aware of, things that God has prepared for those who love him. God has a plan for each one of us and he must reveal it to us when we come to him through the Holy Spirit. It is the work of the Holy Spirit for one to understand the true meaning of scriptures or to share them with other people.

We have the responsibility to preach the word with the help of the Holy Spirit. We cannot brush aside the Holy Spirit and teach the word of God without him. It will be like teaching school children without being trained and authorised to teach by authorised educational institutions. But not only that, the Holy Spirit gives us the power to cast out demons, speak in tongues, trample on serpents and lay hands on the sick for them to be healed. As indicated, there are a lot of things to do pertaining to God's kingdom and we cannot do them without the Holy Spirit. Daily, pray to God and commit everything about your day, into his hands. Put your plans of the day into his hands and let him be the guide of your thoughts, words, and actions. When you do this, you are less likely to make mistakes. You are going to think, talk and work right.

THE HOLY SPIRIT REVEALS OF OUR FUTURE TO US

The future is one of the things God has not revealed to humanity. No one knows the future and what it holds for them. We can attempt to predict the future, but we will not know what comes with it. We may try to predict the future by the plans we have, but we cannot accurately know what will happen. If anything, the future is what gets many people worried about life on Earth in the context of what will happen to them. People have gone as far as seeking Satanic witches and magicians to tell them about their future, but it is always in vain, if they refuse to seek God for understanding. It is only the Holy Spirit who can reveal to us our future.

John 16:13 However, when He, the Spirit of truth, has come, He will guide you into all truth; for He will not speak on His own authority, but whatever He hears He will speak; and He will tell you things to come. NKJV.

Someone may ask, where exactly is this verse talking about the future? In the last part of the verse, "He will tell you things to come." This verse is even here individualised to the one-on-one revelation of things of God to persons who seek the Holy Spirit about their future. There are some things God has hidden from us until we come to him to reveal them to us through the Holy Spirit. If you want to know your future, then you better be a friend of the Holy Spirit.

3

THE GIFTS OF THE HOLY SPIRIT IN YOU

KNOWLEDGE

All of us, as human beings desire to have knowledge but not all of us end up having knowledge. Besides that, the knowledge we have is determined by the source of it, and the resources we commit to it, to acquire it. To be exact we have human knowledge acquired through human source and we have God's knowledge given to us with the help of the Holy Spirit. We can be educated or knowledgeable by the standards of human knowledge given to us by human experts, yet that is not sufficient knowledge at all. If the Earthly knowledge given to us by our human experts, is what we go by, then we will have the most educated group (PHD holders), leading us, in the world today. Despite being educated through the world's education and with the world's knowledge, this group of the most educated people has failed to explain the source of knowledge they have. Well, most human beings have had an unsatisfactory explanation of the source of their knowledge that goes beyond their own natural ideas. And for this reason, they have failed to explain the origin of ideas that are beyond human reasoning. What is the source of these people's ideas? The only book on Earth which has the true explanation about the source of human knowledge is the Bible. People over years have gone into the established worldly education system, yet they have not discovered themselves and the sources of their own knowledge. They have relied on the already established knowledge, but the source of the knowledge, they have no idea about.

Well, the world's knowledge is deeply rooted within Godly knowledge. Knowledge is a gift from God. God is the source of all the knowledge including that of human beings. One important attribute of God is that he is omniscient (all knowing). Which means he is the source of all knowledge including Earthly knowledge. He is the creator of all things including human beings. So, if human beings have knowledge, then it is knowledge from God. In the world for example, we have universal knowledge that applies to all people on Earth whether they have met each other or not. In all cultures across nations, we have the name of God (proving and acknowledging him as the source of all knowledge), languages (we can learn and understand), death ceremonies and rituals (we observe), marriages we conduct (between men and women), all human rights to live and own things, and the knowledge of the environment around us. It is God who is behind all this knowledge available to the people of the world.

Interestingly on the other hand, we can have knowledge about ourselves, and the world around, yet still lack knowledge about God, who gave us our own knowledge. That is the reason people today continue to struggle to explain basic things of God's creation. Yes, indeed some people attempt to explain the origin of things, yet they end up with a lot of assumptions, mistakes, and unexplained parts of the mysteries of creation. By doing this there is aways a void or a vacuum, which is created forcing people to consult the spirits in the spiritual world. When they do this, they either consult God's spirit or Satan's spirit in their quest for knowledge. Again, the knowledge will differ depending on the source of knowledge we consult in the spiritual world. God is the source of truth, and when we consult the spirit of God, we will get the right information about our origin, but when we consult the Satanic source, we will get lies about our origin because he is there to deceive us into his control and dominion. The Devil will be happy to let you have the physical things of this world and not the supernatural things of the spiritual world. So again, Satanic knowledge is always limited. This limited Satanic knowledge can lead to death at the end of our life on Earth because there is no truth in it.

Knowledge is the first gift of the Spirit of God (Holy Spirit), to humanity. Note, it is a gift by the Holy Spirit to you and without him you cannot acquire it. For God to reveal deep things of his kingdom to you, it must be done by his spirit. But again, this does not have to happen unless we have been born again by his spirit, to know the things of God. When we are born by the Holy Spirit, we have our supernatural door opened to knowledge of the things of God. The presence of the Spirit of God within us, activates our own human spirits to receive from the Holy Spirit. The knowledge will flow into our spirits through inner knowledge. The word of knowledge comes to us when we are studying the Bible or other subject matter of concern to us of which we have no understanding, but as we meditate or brainstorm, we can instantly get the answers from inside us, sometimes immediately, or sometimes later. This can come to us in the form of a thought, impression or even the physical environment around us. It can also happen while we are asleep, when an angel of the Lord can be sent to us to teach us about the subject matter through a dream, vision, or a voice. The Spirit of God wants to be our friend and guide. He is willing to guide us in anything and everything such as getting a job, who to marry, understanding the Bible, starting a business, solving family conflicts, your specific assignment in life, preaching the gospel and so much more. There is no other friend I can recommend to you more than the Spirit of God (Holy Spirit).

There are many reasons why we must seek God's knowledge over our own knowledge. God's knowledge is sovereign and unlimited, covering the events of the past, present and future. The Bible is full of information about this knowledge. For example, God knows the hearts of humans and their thoughts including the number of hairs on their heads, he knows all plants and animals of the Earth, he knows the beginning and the end of all things. That is why we must always trust him and what he does. In order to have God's knowledge we must first renounce or reject our own knowledge, for God's knowledge. Despite our current human advancement in education, humanity is still discovering many aspects of God's creation including our bodies, seas and oceans, and the universe around us. It is only God who knows the secrets of people's hearts and that's why we must not hide our sins from him, rather we need to confess them because he knows them anyway. The creator of all things is the giver of all knowledge.

Exodus 31: *¹ Then the Lord spoke to Moses, saying: ² «See, I have called by name Bezalel the son of Uri, the son of Hur, of the tribe of Judah. ³ And I have filled him with the Spirit of God, in wisdom, in understanding, in knowledge, and in all manner of workmanship, ⁴ to design artistic works, to work in gold, in silver, in bronze, ⁵ in cutting jewels for setting, in carving wood, and to work in all manner of workmanship. ⁶ And I, indeed I, have appointed with him Aholiab the son of Ahisamach, of the tribe of Dan; and I have put wisdom in the hearts of all who are gifted artisans, that they may make all that I have commanded you: ⁷ the tabernacle of meeting, the ark of the Testimony and the mercy seat that is on it, and all the furniture of the tabernacle-- ⁸ the table and its utensils, the pure gold lampstand with all its utensils, the altar of incense, ⁹ the altar of burnt offering with all its utensils, and the laver and its base-- ¹⁰ the garments of ministry, the holy garments for Aaron the priest and the garments of his sons, to minister as priests, ¹¹ and the anointing oil and sweet incense for the holy place. According to all that I have commanded you they shall do.» NKJV.*

WISDOM

There are many things God has held back from humanity, and wisdom is one of those things. Many highly educated people today are still struggling in life, because they lack wisdom. There is no institution on Earth in which mankind can be taught wisdom. Wisdom is the main ingredient for applying knowledge. Without wisdom, knowledge is most likely redundant for many people. If we lack wisdom, it can be given to us by God. In fact, it is one of the seven spirits of God. The invitation of the Holy Spirit into your life is also an invitation of wisdom into your life.

Wisdom is referred to as know-how. God's wisdom enables us to know how to do things in life. Wisdom allows one to put in place plans and strategies that enables one to do things in an effective manner. The first deception by Satan took place in the garden of Eden to Adam and Eve, and it was about their desire for wisdom. Unfortunately, out of their desire for wisdom they got deceived and perished because they were seeking wisdom in wrong places and from the wrong source. Wisdom is the desire for every man and woman, but we do not always get it because we look for it in the wrong places.

God does not need your knowledge. It is of no help to him. He did not give you knowledge for you to help him but rather, to help yourself and your fellow human beings. He provides you with knowledge, abilities and skills to understand hard things of men to help your fellow men and women. If you want to know things of God, you must first shun your human wisdom. You must approach things of God through the position of need, not the position of satisfaction. There is no PhD, master's degree and Degree, which will enable you to know things of God. God hates the proud and He only teaches the humble. So, let no one boast in himself or others. If there were no challenges beyond human wisdom, we would not need God at all. Humans don't like death, war, disease and poverty, but those things exist, and they can do nothing about them. They continue to challenge our human wisdom and as such continue prove to us that we need God in our lives as human beings.

So, this begs the question, what part does human wisdom play in solving all these challenges against our very existence? The wisdom of men comes to nothing if they are hits by sicknesses, natural disasters, accidents, and other human challenges. You do not need to wait to be hit by one of the above disasters to know there is a God. Before you have to face a desperate situation and now is the time to believe in him.

God can only show up in the affairs of human beings, when their wisdom is completely exhausted. You can be educated but still live a miserable life if you are not with God. Here is the reason you need God throughout your life; he has held back his wisdom, knowledge, revelation and understanding to be accessible only by those who wholeheartedly seek him and love him. That is why you can have your education but remain helpless without his wisdom to apply what you have learned, daily regarding difficult matters of life.

Isaiah 55:8-12 "For My thoughts are not your thoughts ,Nor are your ways My ways," says the Lord." For as the heavens are higher than the Earth, So are My ways higher than your ways, And My thoughts than your thoughts." For as the rain comes down, and the snow from heaven, And do not return there, But water the Earth, And make it bring forth and bud, That it may give seed to the Sower And bread to the eater, So shall My word be that goes forth from My mouth; It shall not return to Me void, But it shall accomplish what I please, And it shall prosper in the thing for which I sent it. "For you shall go out with joy and be led out with peace; The mountains and the hills Shall break forth into singing before you, and all the trees of the field shall clap their hands. NKJV.

The mysteries of God's kingdom simply beat humanity's

logic and wisdom. God has framed everything he has created through his wisdom. All things work together and are there in their places of order because of God's wisdom. With Godly wisdom, we can do things quickly with little effort and time. It would be better for us to use our God given wisdom in applying the knowledge we have acquired through our education. The one who has wisdom has precious treasure that has better value than gold, silver, and bronze. He who has wisdom has what it takes to acquire principles that enables him to accumulate wealth. He who has wisdom has better ideas and better ways of producing products and services that are competitive in the market. He who has wisdom always inspires a crowd of followers to a cause of life. He who has wisdom has good admonition that can save lives, time, energy and money for that matter.

Wisdom is sometimes associated with old age but that is not always necessarily the case. You can be old and still be foolish and you can be young and be wise. This is not to discredit the elders, because there is always experience, knowledge and wisdom acquired over years by many elders that make most of them wiser than young people. However, even if we find ourselves having wisdom, it is not advisable that we brag about it, without doing anything with it. Sometimes we may be perceived as fools if we talk about our own wisdom, without welcoming counsel from others.

Intriguingly, there were people who had no fame, knowledge or power, but they were able to preach the word of God to people. Most Jesus' disciples were fishermen and tax-collectors, yet they were able to convince men and women to follow Christ through their teachings. They drew to themselves large crowds of people who were convinced by their wise teaching.

Throughout their ministries they relied on God's wisdom to preach the word. They were they cleverest than the most educated people of the world because of the Holy Spirit. That is why St. Paul says in the book of (1 Corinthians 1:18), that the foolishness of God is wiser than the wisdom of man. Being from the lower class of society, yet they were able to challenge the most educated group of Pharisees and Sadducees, on spiritual doctrines. Those who think they are wise, are fools, when it comes to the knowledge of things of God. Foolish people do not realise they are foolish, so they continue to perish in their foolishness. People continue to go to hell because of their lack of knowledge of God We must make ourselves fools to inherit the kingdom of God.

Proverbs 1:7 The fear of the Lord is the beginning of knowledge, but fools despise wisdom and instruction. NKJV.

We are advised to seek wisdom when we do not have it. How many people are killed today in the world because of their reckless speech? How many products and services are not in the market today because of people's poor plans and poor strategies? How many families are separated today because of people's selfishness and self-righteousness? You can see, lack of wisdom can be costly and deadly to human society. Because we have rejected God, he has held back his wisdom from humanity. People have rejected the Bible today, yet it is the only book that is full of wisdom. Because it was written by great men and women of God, who were leaders and at the same time great servants of God, who by help of the Holy Spirit, were inspired to lead and write. No one has read the Bible and remains a fool. James has put it very clearly that, if we lack wisdom then, we must seek it from God, who is willing to freely give it to us (James 3:17).

James 3: ⁱ⁷ *But the wisdom that is from above is first pure, then peaceable, gentle, willing to yield, full of mercy and good fruits, without partiality and without hypocrisy. NKJV.*

The wisdom from God is always pure, peace-loving, merciful, unwavering, gentle and without pretense, whereas the human wisdom breaks us down and tears us apart. Human wisdom is always full of deception, lying, accusations and division. When we have Godly wisdom, our intentions are always pure and non-destructive to other people. What we do is always based in love of others and the love of God. A wisdom that rejects God, and his creation is not of God, but a Satanic wisdom. Anything that a person does with an intention to destroy his fellow human beings is worldly and Satanic in nature.

We learn from the Bible that King Solomon was very wise and received his wisdom from God after he asked for it. We know that Solomon was a son of the previous famous King in Israel who was also a very rich man called King David. So, Solomon had riches he inherited from his father, and he could have asked for more material resources. But he knew that without wisdom the material riches and power could be easily lost. And so, he chose to ask God for wisdom to lead his people., This was not a common thing, because not many people before him, including his own father, had asked for wisdom. Solomon knew very well that asking for wisdom is an invitation of God into the affairs of Israel and his leadership. His actions pleased God, and God gave Solomon wisdom with many material blessings thereafter.

The world is crumbling today because it has rejected the wisdom of God. How many people go to church today? How many people pray and fast today? How many people have Bibles in their homes today and read them daily? How many people today acknowledge God as the creator of the universe? With these questions in mind, you will realise that most people have lost knowledge of God due to their worldly commitments. In Australia for example, most of the people you find in churches are the elderly who are less than 10% of the population of Australia according to many research studies. That means almost 90% of Australians do not go to church. You will find a lot of people today at the beach or sporting events rather than in the Churches. This majority of people in Australia, have lost the wisdom of God. Every human life has its challenges and situations that need wisdom to be tackled. Wisdom determines the success of one's life and no one can make progress in this life without wisdom. The Bible says that people are destroyed because of lack of knowledge of God.

PROPHECY

The gift of prophecy is one of the most important gifts of the Holy Spirit. It is the greatest gift that every person should desire because it brings to us the information about the future that is hidden from us by God. Blessed is he who can hear God's voice bring back to us the message of God and the instructions in which it can be carried out. There is nothing greater beyond the fact that one can get direct and clear messages from God, on the behalf of the individual, community, society and the nation, in order to encourage, edify, exhorts, comfort and build up people's hope.

On the other hand, the gift of prophecy is not without controversy, because of its abuse and the misrepresentation by those who are given it. One primary reason for its controversy is whether God has spoken or not, and if he has spoken, is it accurate enough for people to believe? Firstly, to test whether the prophecy is accurate enough, it must scriptural. Secondly it must come to pass, and if it doesn't, then it is a false prophecy.

1 Corinthians 14: [1] Pursue love, and desire spiritual gifts, but especially that you may prophesy. [2] For he who speaks in a tongue does not speak to men but to God, for no one understands him; however, in the spirit he speaks mysteries. [3] But he who prophesies speaks edification and exhortation and comfort to men. [4] He who speaks in a tongue edifies himself, but he who prophesies edifies the church. [5] I wish you all spoke with tongues, but even more that you prophesied; for he who prophesies is greater than he who speaks with tongues, unless indeed he interprets, that the church may receive edification. NKJV.

"THE OFFICE OF PROPHETIC"

The office of the prophetic deals with a person, people, communities, societies and nations in the foretelling of their future by God through the prophets. God communicates with the prophets through the voice, visions and dreams, words of knowledge, sounds and many signs and wonders they receive from God and declare to the people. The office of prophecy deals with future events only, as God shows the prophets what will happen in the future in the human society.

So far so good, but what is very controversial is who among the prophets God speaks to and who speak back to God? Who among the prophets declared the word of God to the people as it was given? Who among the prophets lies to people out of the fantasy that he speaks to God? Who among the prophets is being used by the Devil to lie to them about their future? Stay with me now as we distinguish them here:

WHO ARE THE TRUE PROPHETS?

True prophets of God are God's spokespersons on the behalf of the people. God trusts them and they trust God. True prophets of God receive the word of God and declare it to people as it is given, that which must come to pass. The true prophets of God acknowledge the Holy Spirit, as the power behind the miracles they perform and the words of inspiration they give to people. And more importantly, the true prophets of God condemn human sins in individuals, communities, societies and nations.

WHO ARE THE FALSE PROPHETS?

False prophets are people who claim that God speaks to them, and they must speak to people on God's behalf, yet their message is contrary to God's message. False prophets can also be defined as people who claim the gift of prophecy or divine inspiration to speak for God, yet they are under the influence of the Devil. The Devil shows them misguided visions and dreams that do not come to pass or if they do come to pass, then there must strings attached, like payment of money and selling of your souls. False prophets will point people to themselves, other gods, and to theories aimed at deviating people away from the true God of Heaven. False prophets will never condemn human sins as they themselves practise a sinful lifestyle.

As we have seen in the bible, false prophets and false prophecy is not a thing of the recent past but has existed through human history. False prophets, whether they are under the influence of the Devil or out of their fantasy, have the following motivations: desire for power, influence, control, prestige, and money and sexual desires over human beings. They have no love for people in their hearts.

WHO ARE FALSE TEACHERS?

False Teachers are people who no longer follow the laws, statutes and commandments of God with regards to Christian ways of worship instituted and given to us by God. They have instead through their religions produced their own rules, and hymns for worship. This has caused more confusion in the churches of God today than worship itself. Let us look at the true doctrines versus false doctrines here; true doctrines originate from God and are grounded in the Bible whereas false doctrines originate with humans and are not grounded in the Bible.

False teachers are also prevalent today in our human society just as they have been in the past. In this age of rebellion and intolerance against God and his laws, false teachers have multiplied and are exploiting the situation. This has produced an easy-going religion that is oblivious to sin, and which requires no effort and commitment to God and the punishment of sins. As this generation of end-time people wants to live without the condemnation of their sin, many leaders have avoided talking about sins in their sermons. Some of our Christian's faith leaders have even removed laws of God governing the Christian ways of worship in their dominations. In some dominations today, there has been the introduction of new laws in the areas of marriage, worship, wealth accumulation, and power control. Many dominations and their teachers have come out very openly in support of same-sex marriage, abortion, pornography and climate change, creating the perversion of God's laws.

False Teachers can be those who acknowledge themselves as a substitute of Jesus Christ on Earth in their dominations. Or perhaps those who deny Jesus Christ as the son of God and the only way to heaven. Or those who claim to speak to God yet deny the holy spirit as the connection to God. Or those who think marriage should accommodate any lifestyle. Or those who think their dominations are better than others and are the only way to heaven. Or those who think it is normal to kill the unborn child in the mother's womb. Hence there are many false teachers in the world today, more than there have been in the past as the world is reaching the age of maturity of sins. In a nutshell, false teaching comes from man or Satan and is aimed at pulling people away from God, particularly in these end-times days. This false teaching has produced spiritually unhealthy, ignorant and immature Christians who are not Christians at all and are destined to lose their salvation.

In nutshell, false prophets and false teachers are doing one thing, and that is to pull you away from God in order that you lose your salvation. Their source of power is either from the demons or themselves. They are all interested in getting power, wealth, prestige and popularity that make them look better in the eyes of people.

You have the responsibility to accept and hold fast to what is true and deny what is false. We must also be vigilant with those prophets and teachers to discern whether they can acknowledge the holy spirit, Jesus Christ and God as the only way for salvation. We must stick to the bible as a guideline in what we think, speak and do, in order not to be lost at this defining moment of the end times. More importantly, the churches and the Christians in them must stick to the bible and welcome those who teach sound doctrines and reject or rebuke those who teach false doctrines about the lordship of Jesus Christ, who is the head of the Christian church.

FAITH

Without faith, you cannot please God. The non-Christians walks by sight, and Christians walks by faith. God is a spirit, and we cannot see spirit with our own naked eyes. Although we are spirits as mankind, we have a body that hinders our spiritual eyes from seeing spiritual things or other spirit beings. Hence, the spirits do see us, but we don't see the spirits so long as we are in this human body. It is only when we die and leave this human body that our spirit beings will see other spirits including the spirit of God. The only way we can see spirits is through faith, believing that spirits do exist, including God, who is a spirit.

It is by faith believing that the spirits do exist, and they can communicate to us that warrant the spirits to speak to us. The first spirit that would have an encounter with us if we believed and are baptised by it, is the Holy Spirit of God. It is this spirit, which connects us to the other spirits, namely angelic spiritual beings, our Lord Jesus Christ, and God almighty.

Your faith is intertwined with your miracle. There can never be a miracle without faith in God. Your level of faith in God determines your miracle. God is after his glory and there are some conditions. He will allow the doctors to treat us if he thinks we are going to discredits his glory of healing us. All most all the human sufferings are caused by our choices that we make without God. To that effect, all human sufferings are an invitation by God for humanity to seek him.

The good news is that all of us have been given by God the measure of faith with which to operate. Not only have we been given faith to be saved, but we have also been given faith to carry out our daily activities. There are some things we do today, knowing tomorrow by faith we will have them. Undoubtedly, we go to school to study with the faith that we will have a job in the future, when we are young, we have faith that we will one day marry and make families of our own, when we open our business we have faith that we will make money, we plant our crops and we have faith that they will grow. We plan with the faith that we will live and, we go to bed every day with the faith that we will wake up in the morning, and the list goes on and on. Thus, you can see that God has already given us a measure of faith to do our own things, and without this faith we can do nothing.

Furthermore, when we walk with God over time, our faith becomes the cornerstone of everything we do. Faith becomes our licence to draw our blessings from God. Nothing pleases God more than to see you have unwavering faith in him. Faith becomes your lifestyle. The Bible says, the just shall live by faith (Romans 1:17). God has an assurance of resources and victories for those who live by faith in him. Faith is a shield of defence against the wicked people in the world. Whatever a person plans against you and your family shall never prosper because of your faith in God. Your faith can bring down every Satanic arrow, whether it is sickness, poverty, unemployment, jealousy, lying, hatred, violence, drunkenness, envy, and all forms of oppression.

There are great men and great stories of faith in the Bible we can always refer to if we are going through difficult challenges in life. Abraham was credited by God as the father of faith because of the number of tests he passed. Perhaps the biggest test was when he was asked by God to sacrifice his only son to God. Think about it. He had waited for the child for nearly twenty-five years, and after having the child, God asked, Abraham to sacrifice him. Many people would have said, not me, God, I am not doing it for you. But Abraham went ahead and obeyed the demand of God. Many people are still asking today, Why did God do this? Well, he was doing it to strengthen the faith of Abraham in him. God just wanted to see whether Abraham would have a different reaction to God after having the previous gift from him. He wanted to see whether Abraham would prioritise Isaac over God. There are no records in human history nor is there any verse in the Bible which talks about an instance of which God demanded children to be sacrificed to him. This was what made Abraham the great father of faith, knowing his God very well and what he is capable of; he knew that God could raise Isaac from death even if he had killed him. God in return was pleased with Abraham's faith and released all Abraham provisions. Abraham's faith was justified and validated by his actions. What we say and what we do must match in order to please God.

Abraham's faith in God reminds us that we must have the same faith in God. Our words must match our actions. What we say, we must do so that God can trust us. God is after his glory, and he cannot work with people who cannot acknowledge him and his great work in them. This is the reason why we must work individually. Our work determines the tangible fruits of our actions, not our words. What we say, must practically produce results for people to see, so that they can have the same faith in God. Sometimes people want to see the results of our faith not the words of our faith. God wants to partner with us so that what he wants to do, he can do through us. That is why he tests people to see whether they are trustworthy, and obedient to him in order not to claim credit for what he has done through them.

Think about this, if there is no one on Earth who is representing God, how will other people know he exists? How will he reach out to other people in need or help? How will we know the dangers we may face in the future? Just as it was then to Abraham and other great men and women of faith, God wants to reach out to people today through us who are willing and obedient to carry out his mission on Earth. God is today looking for his obedient and willing servants who are readily available for the end times harvest. God wants people to be saved, but they cannot be saved without people who are willing to preach the gospel to them. Are you ready to step up for God's mission today?

Hebrews 11: [1] Now faith is the substance of things hoped for, the evidence of things not seen. [2] For by it the elders obtained a good testimony. [3] By faith we understand that the worlds were framed by the word of God, so that the things which are seen were not made of things which are visible. [4] By faith Abel offered to God a more excellent sacrifice than Cain, through which he obtained witness that he was righteous, God testifying of his gifts; and through it he being dead still speaks. ⁵ By faith Enoch was taken away so that he did not see death, «and was not found, because God had taken him»; for before he was taken he had this testimony, that he pleased God. ⁶ But without faith it is impossible to please Him, for he who comes to God must believe that He is, and that He is a rewarder of those who diligently seek Him. ⁷ By faith Noah, being divinely warned of things not yet seen, moved with godly fear, prepared an ark for the saving of his household, by which he condemned the world and became heir of the righteousness which is according to faith. ⁸ By faith Abraham obeyed when he was called to go out to the place which he would receive as an inheritance. And he went out, not knowing where he was going. NKJV.

HEALINGS

Certainly, our healing is guaranteed by God. This was spoken through the prophet Isaiah 700 years before our Lord Jesus Christ came into the world. *Isaiah 53:4 Surely, He has borne our griefs and carried our sorrows; Yet we esteemed Him stricken, Smitten by God, and afflicted. 5 But He was wounded for our transgressions, He was bruised for our iniquities; The chastisement for our peace was upon Him, And by His stripes we are healed.*

One of the painful things we continue to experience today as Christians even after this promised of healing, is the fact that we continue to be afflicted with sicknesses in our bodies by the Devil, because we do not know how to claim our free healing. Almost all the diseases we are afflicted with, in our bodies today, have their roots in the spiritual world. In the Satanic Kingdom there is a spirit assigned to cause diseases on the human bodies, called the "Spirit of Infirmity."

Luke 13:10 Now He was teaching in one of the synagogues on the Sabbath. 11 And behold, there was a woman who had a spirit of infirmity eighteen years and was bent over and could in no way raise herself up. 12 But when Jesus saw her, He called her to Him and said to her, "Woman, you are loosed from your infirmity." 13 And He laid His hands on her, and immediately she was made straight, and glorified God.

If diseases were not rooted in the Spiritual world, God would have not made this promise of healing through Isaiah. This woman in the book of Luke had suffered from the Spirit of infirmity which had crippled her for eighteen years. She was physically bent at her back, but no one could believe that it was the work of a demonic Spirit until God came and revealed it to us. It is not that woman alone, but many of us today continue to be attacked by the same demon, yet we are not aware of it. We struggle with physical symptoms, yet we do not know that there are spirits behind them, making us sick.

Healing is one of the important gifts of the Holy Spirit. No one has the ability to cast out demons without the presence of the Spirit of God within him. It is the Spirit of God that casts out demons from people who are not the servants of God. God just needs our bodies to heal the sick. Knowing that we are sick because of the demonic spirit, he sent us his spirit to live with us forever to heal us from demonic spirits. Jesus Christ was the first person to cast out demons in people distinguishing the Kingdom of God from the Kingdom of Satan. After this, the gift of healing was given to everyone who believes in God and is baptised by the Holy Spirit. Even as God has given us the gift of healing the sick, we have no monopoly as the Spirit still chooses who gets healed at that time, and who does not. It is important to emphasise so that you do not get disappointed if the people you have prayed for are not healed. I have had instances in which I prayed for people, and some got healed and some did not get healed. I was always disappointed for those that did not get healed because of the terrible condition they are in. When they didn't get healed, I used to blame myself thinking that I was doing something wrong, and that I had hindered their healing. But this is not true. I was wrong, God has a choice of who to heal and at what time, due to what is happening in their lives, I was not aware of. That is why we need to get the facts right about what is happening in people's lives before we can administer healing to them. Sometimes people may not get healed because of their lack of faith, unforgiveness, doubt or unrepented sin. It has nothing to do with God or the person administering the healing.

A story is told in the Bible about the woman with the issue of blood, as a good example of how the Spirit of God directly heals people. The woman had gone through many painful doctors' treatments, but she was not healed. She was drained of all her resources, but it was all in vain. She suffered at the hands of physicians while seeking treatment that made her condition even worse, yet they took all her money. Why didn't she get healed by the doctors? Well, the doctors never knew that there was a demon behind her condition. Her condition was abnormal not to believe that there was a demonic affliction behind it. The doctors just dealt with the symptoms and not the root causes of her sickness. She was terribly failed by the medical field, yet they took away all her money and left her in poverty even if she was to be healed through them. That is what the Devil does; when he strikes us with diseases, he wants us to be left in poverty, if not death for that matter. It was very clear that the woman was never going to receive her healing until the spirit behind her condition was dealt with. While she was seeking treatment, she was also seeking God's intervention in her case. While Jesus was passing by, she was positioned by the Holy Spirit to get heal. This was indicated by her strong faith in God, and upon touching the fringes of the garment of the Lord Jesus Christ, she was instantly healed of her condition. God is our answer; where humans failed, God always succeeded. Instantly the fountain of blood that had flowed out of her for twelve years was dried up.

Hope at time of trials is putting our expectations above ourselves – that which we cannot control, can be controlled somewhere by a supernatural being who is beyond our imagination and our understanding. It is easy to lose hope if things we put our hope in, have been totally ruined by forces beyond our control. Sometimes things such as family relationships, health, finances, jobs, homes, power, business, friendship and so much more, are the things we based our hope on, and when they are lost, we become hopeless, losing our meaning in life and sense of direction. The risk of putting our hope in things we own or the things we anticipate having in the future or in other people, is that when they are lost, we can quickly fall into hopelessness, depression and in extreme cases, suicide.

But this is totally different with Christians because we put our hope in God who is our creator and the controller of all things that comes our ways. The Bible says, "cursed is the man who puts his hope in another man." Many Christians know that whether good or bad, all things work together for good to those who love God. The Bible tells us that we cannot hope in things we see but the things we do not see, for the hope that is seen is not a hope at all. The trials we go through as Christians are there not to destroy us but rather to bring out the hope in us not to trust in ourselves but our Lord Jesus Christ. The trials in our lives are in fact opportunity for us to know God. Once we meet God, we are assured that our problems will be solved, then we can relax and rejoice as we wait patiently for our answers from him. But not only that, there is no temptation which has overtaken us, which has not been before, and will not be in the future. All the trials we are going through have been gone through by other people before us and will come to other people who will come after us in the future. But above all God is the Lord over all these things. So, we should relax and let God take control of our situations or conditions. All we must do is to have faith, trust, and hope in God, as he is master of all miracles, and he may turn our situation around for the better if we had sought him and stuck with him. The hope we have beyond ourselves should be the hope we must anchored our trust in. This hope in God should be the light at the end of the tunnel, for us no matter what comes our way, while waiting for the Lord answers. So long as you are alive, know that God is not done with you. Never give up on God, he will respond no matter what. Know this, there is nothing impossible with our God. He is the Lord over all the impossibilities of mankind. Soldier on with the good fight of faith.

MIRACLES

In the words of the great man of God, John Hagee, in one of his sermons said, "the miracle is in your Mouth." What you believe in your heart (Your Spirit) and speak using your mouth will come to pass. The mistake is to give up your entire future because of the current situation you are going through. No condition is permanent. Every bad thing that comes your way does not come to destroy but to build you up. If it was to destroy you, God would have not allowed it to happen to you. Every potential to defeat whatever you are going through is within you. Your life is not over so long as you are alive. There is no disease which God cannot healed.

In fact, miracle working is a gift of the Holy Spirit to every man and woman who seeks him. There is nothing impossible with God if you can believe. Let me tell you this; God is the creator of all things and there is nothing that is impossible with him. Before that challenge came to you, he knew it already. Certainly, our Lord Jesus Christ, was heavily used by the Spirit of God, when he was here on Earth because he had made himself available to be used. God can use any man or woman, so long as they are willing to surrender their lives to him. God is looking for people who are obedient and willing to be used by him. God needs those he can send to reach out to other people who need miraculous healing in their bodies or in their other situations or conditions.

Indeed, a miracle is an unexpected supernatural intervention of God in our situation. The miracle is called as such because it is an unexpected change in our situation without our understanding. It happens when God overrules the forces of darkness working against us, in the background of our situation. There are numerous examples in the Bible where people were healed unexpectedly by the Holy Spirit in Jesus, such as the Centurion's servant, the paralytic, Peter's mother in-law, the man born blind at birth, and the lame man at the pool in Bethesda. All these people got healed because of their faith in God.

Furthermore, your faith in God is critical to your healing. Unless you have faith, you cannot please God. God has already given you a measure of faith to work with. Jesus puts it very clear here in the book of Mark 10: [22]

So Jesus answered and said to them, «Have faith in God. [23] For assuredly, I say to you, whoever says to this mountain, ‹Be removed and be cast into the sea,' and does not doubt in his heart, but believes that those things he says will be done, he will have whatever he says. [24] Therefore I say to you, whatever things you ask when you pray, believe that you receive them, and you will have them. NKJV.

There is a lot of information in these verses that needs to be unpacked, but firstly Christ is telling us here that we must have faith in God. Faith that acknowledges that God exists, and he can hear our prayers. Faith that speaks against whatever we are going through that was never part of us and cannot be part of us going forward. Speaking against the mountain, means speaking against every heavy condition or situation we are in, and we have no power or authority to get rid of. When you speak against whatever you are going through without doubt in your heart, believing that what you have spoken against cannot long exist with you, then you can have what you want. Very impressive indeed. So, speak and believe and you will have it.

Besides that, our miracle is also tied to the sins we have

committed prior. Can I tell you these demons do not just attack people randomly, there must be a justification for their attack, otherwise God would not allow them to attack you. This may not be necessarily the case always, but a lot of people who do not receive their healing when great men and women of God pray for them, miss out due to their unconfessed sins that have given the demons legal rights to be in them. There would have been a door opened for the demons to come into their life. These can include among other things, adultery, injustice, violence, bloodshed, idol worship, offenses, anger, and generational curses. I must emphasise this; unconfessed sins are a strong reason for demons' legal rights. The demons can remain in you until you have confessed the sins which got them into you in the first place. If you know any sin you have committed before you got into the problem you are going through, then you must confess it. There is no point in hiding it from God because he knows it anyway. Just confess it and receive your miracle; this is the way to your freedom forever. There is no sin God cannot forgive. This must be good news to you; when your sins are forgiven, God is able to cleanse you of all unrighteousness. Even in an ideal family setting, if you are a married man or woman, you would love that child who always admits his or her sins before you can confront them, more than the one that hides them.

1 John 1:8 If we say that we have no sin, we deceive ourselves, and the truth is not in us. 9 If we confess our sins, He is faithful and just to forgive us our sins and to cleanse us from all unrighteousness. 10 If we say that we have not sinned, we make Him a liar, and His word is not in us. NKJV.

In addition, your miracle is tied to your willingness and

your obedience to what God wants you to do. At times we go through problems to wake us up, for God called in our lives. We can sometimes come under attack because we are sitting over God's assignment in our lives. We go through a series of tests because God is preparing us for his future assignment. God intentionally allows us to go through a series of battles with demonic powers, to prepare us for future battles that may come our way after our miracle. When you have gone through many battles and won, God will use them for his future glory for those who may go through similar situations in the future. The battles you have won become future testimonies for future generations. By these battles you earn enough experiences to teach future generations how to win their future battles.

While you wait for your miracle you must be patient, knowing that God is in control, and he will bring your miracle to pass. When you are waiting for your miracle, it is a time to read the Bible, pray, fast, and listen to the other preachers of the word and practise listening to voice of God, not complaining, and blaming God for your problems. There is nothing God hates like a complainer, who wants everything done quickly for him or her. You know why God hates complainers? Because they doubt the power of God to bring them their miracles. God will never bring your miracle to pass based on your terms and your time, but on his terms and his time.

DISCERNMENT

Your ability to know what is happening around you is spiritually given to you by God. Before things manifest in the physical dimension, they first happen in the spiritual dimension. The planning and communication of what will happen to you in the natural world will have first occurred in the supernatural world. Whether it is God's plan for you or Satan's plan against you, it must first occur in the spiritual world. That is why you need the gift of discernment of spirits, to know which spirits are talking to you or for that matter, attacking you.

What happened to Job still happens to us today. What happened to Job had to happen first in the spiritual world before the physical world. There was a conversation about Job in the spiritual arena between God and Satan. Job obviously was a faithful servant of God, sinless, God fearing and living righteously before God. Satan did not like the character and the lifestyle of Job, because it was a good example to those at his time and to those who would come after him, that Satan would want to destroy through sins in the future. He went to God to ask God to remove his protection hedges around Job, to attack him and see whether Job would continue to fear and live a sinless life before God. God, knowing Job very well, had to grant Satan permission to attack Job and not to kill him. All these conversations happened in the spiritual world before the can happen in the natural would. When a person lives a lifestyle that is free from sins, Satan will do nothing to him. For him to own you, he must get you to commit sin, to negate God's protective hedges around you.

What happened in the spirit now had to happen in the physical or natural world. Job came under the attacks of Satan in many ways. Satan started attacking him physically by killing all Job's children, raids (through foreign raiders) all Job's livelihoods or resources (animals), attacked his body with diseases (boils), influenced Job's wife to get Job to curse God and die, and finally got Job's friends to accused him of the uncommitted sins against God, to justify the reasons he was under Satanic attacks.

As Job received the simultaneous news of the destruction of his family and properties, he had to use the Spirit of discernment to know that he was under Satanic attack. He immediately knew that he was under Satanic attack and so he had to run to God and humble himself before God, seeking protection. While seeking God protection, Job begun fighting-off Satanic attacks by tearing-off his clothes, shaving his head and falling to the ground and worshipping God. He first had to admit that he had lost everything, but he could not lose God. Why was it so important for Job not to lose God in such a scale of destruction? Job knew very well that what happened was allowed by God and it was only God who could restore his family and his property. But more importantly, Job knew that there was something more precious than his family and his property that he must not let go of, and that was his salvation.

Job 1:20 Then Job arose, tore his robe, and shaved his head; and he fell to the ground and worshipped. 21 And he said: "Naked I came from my mother's womb, and naked shall I return there. The Lord gave, and the Lord has taken away; Blessed be the name of the Lord." 22 In all this Job did not sin nor charge God with wrong. NKJV.

The spirit of discernment was not only important for Job to identify and fight his enemy, but we also still need it today if we are to succeed in spiritual warfare. For us to fight the right battles we must have the ability to discern the Holy Spirit and Demonic spirits besides our own human spirits. Because it is the Spirit of God who gives us this ability to discerned spirits,

He will train us and equip us with enough knowledge needed to discern the Demonic spirits from God's Angelic Spirits.

Discerning Demonic Spirits is critical if we are to win against them. The gift of discernment is very important in knowing the types of Demonic spirits who are living inside or outside of us, that are attacking us on daily basis. Unless you have ability to know which type of spirit you are dealing with, you will never win against the demonic spirits. While fighting them inside you or outside, you must call them out by name for them to leave. We know that demons do not enter people's bodies without legal rights to be in there. These legal rights could range from: Satanic covenants, children dedicated to the devil, sexual immorality, bloodshed, idol worship, greed, jealousy, offenses, drunkenness, adultery, lying, stealing and the list goes on. Once they are in there they cannot leave until the legal rights are identified and dealt with by the person. There are many ways in which you might know whether a person is demon-possessed; the demon might speak through the person, their health or property, give them bad thoughts, or leave a toxic smell.

Discerning God's Spirits. The gift of discernment is also important for communication with God Spirits, including the Holy Spirit. The shocking truth today is that many people do not believe that God speaks to us, as mankind. It is just a handful of people who still communicate with heaven today, yet we are all given the ability by God to communicate with him since the restoration of mankind back to God. God's angels are visiting us on daily basis, and we need the ability to recognise them and talk back to them. When the Holy Spirt and heavenly Angels visit or speak to us, we will feel inner peace from the Holy Spirit, indicating to us that these are angels of God. The heavenly angels speak to us through; dreams, visions, voices, word of knowledge and sense of fire that we normally feel around our bodies.

Discerning Human Spirits. We need this spirit of discernment to know what is happening within our bodies, souls, and spirits. Our human spirits and souls are also a source of our problems if they are not managed well. What always gives demonic powers or spirits leeway to get to us, are our human spirits and souls. There must be something out of control within us that will give demonic powers gateway of entry into our bodies. Unless we can discern what is going on within us, we can easily be destroyed by the Devil. The human body has no ability to do good, no matter what the person thinks they are doing right to serve God.

This is one of the reasons among others that we need God for salvation. It is shockingly profound, that the body has no ability to do good because there is nothing good in it that enables it to do so. It was created by God as a corruptible body that has no ability to do good. And every time it attempts to do good, the dictates and confines of it does not allow it to do good by itself, because of the law of sin and death pronounced over it in the garden of Eden by God. So, it is the law of sin and death pronounced over it, that enables the body to have the propensity to commit sin, which always leads to death without God. This happened in the garden of Eden because man violated the instructions of God, testing his willingness and obedience of him not to eat from the tree of knowledge of good and evil. The violation caused him to die and be permanently isolated from God. This is called the law of slavery to sin, leading to death. So, in short, because of Adam and Eve, we are born into slavery of sin, leading to death without God. When a man or woman decides to do things without God, no matter how they may seem to be good to them in their own eyes, they are committing the sin of lawlessness leading to death.

The only way your body can do good is the presence of God in it, in the form of the Holy Spirit, dictating it to do good. The law of life has come from God to give your body the ability to do good and to have life in it again. This is called the law of righteousness to God. So, your ability to do the right thing by God is enabled by the Spirit of God's presence in you. Furthermore, for you to be saved, you must be born of the Spirit of God, the Holy Spirit.

This is why the current world we live in is so broken because we have taken laws into our own hands by rejecting God. Just as Adam did and had nothing to restore him, we are also heading in the same direction, from which nothing can save us. Every time a person rejects God, he is knowingly or unknowingly inviting Satan to be the master of his affairs. The law of sin in mankind attracts Satan, and he capitalised on it to steal, kill, and destroy as many souls as possible without God's intervention.

St. John categorised our human sins into, lust of flesh, lust of the eyes and pride of life (1 john 2:16). These things can destroy us before demons come to attack us. We must always keep them in check if we are to succeed in doing God's work. The Holy Spirit will always give us a flashlight if we are about to go off-course in our mission.

If this is, you then you must change the cause of your life before it is too late because God is still willing to save you. Never seek help from the sons of man on important matters of your life, they have no ability to help.

SPEAKING IN TONGUES

The ability to speak in tongues is a gift of the Holy Spirit. The gift of the tongues is divided into two; the tongue to speak the various languages of people of Earth and the tongue to speak the language of angels of heaven. The ability to speak various human languages is the greater gift of the Holy Spirit. In comparison with speaking the language of angels, there is no risk associated with speaking foreign languages so long as we can learn them and speak them. Imagine if God had not given us the ability to learn various human languages, we would be in isolation from one continent to another in the world today. For example, there would be no understanding of each other's words and their intentions, there would be no trade of goods and services, there would be no intercultural marriages, there would be no resolutions of conflict and diplomatic international relations, and more importantly there would be no sharing and preaching of words of God to various nations of the world. We have today various members of the diplomatic corps who can speak various languages across nations, making sure that the relationship between nations is peaceful and smooth, and missionaries who are preaching the word of God across nations- because of these abilities of the tongues.

Likewise, it is important to point out that in the beginning, when God created the first man Adam, Adam had one language, but this was short lived as he joined Satan in the rebellion against God. There was one language on Earth right until the tower of Babel was built by Nimrod, who was the head of the rebellion against God. One language and one mission by people who were united for the purpose of toppling God from this throne again through the influenced of Satan. This was the second attempt on his throne, and that became a concern for God. This was without doubt the second attempt by Satan to topple God using his union with mankind. Satan hates the fact that the people God created, had replaced him in the custodianship of Earth, and had joined him in the rebellion against God. In as much as there may have been a physical tower built by Nimrod, humanity's united thoughts in building a tower that would reach heaven, was an attempt to be like God. That is exactly what Satan did in heaven before he was cast to Earth. Their attempt to build a tower that could reach heaven and the subsequent response by God to confuse their language indicates that they were able to work against God. That is what Satan continues to do today; he continues to convince mankind to do their work independently of God. Everything that a person does on Earth without consultation with God is illegal and is subject to destruction by God. Every thought that is not inclusive of God in our spirits and souls is an evil thought that will anger God to destruction of mankind.

Genesis 11: [1] *Now the whole Earth had one language and one speech.* [2] *And it came to pass, as they journeyed from the east, that they found a plain in the land of Shinar, and they dwelt there.* [3] *Then they said to one another, «Come, let us make bricks and bake them thoroughly.» They had brick for stone, and they had asphalt for mortar.* [4] *And they said, «Come, let us build ourselves a city, and a tower whose top is in the heavens; let us make a name for ourselves, lest we be scattered abroad over the face of the whole Earth.»* [5] *But the Lord came down to see the city and the tower which the sons of men had built.* [6] *And the Lord said, «Indeed the people are one and they all have one language, and this is what they begin to do; now nothing that they propose to do will be withheld from them. ⁷ Come, let Us go down and there confuse their language, that they may not understand one another›s speech.» ⁸ So the Lord scattered them abroad from there over the face of all the Earth, and they ceased building the city. ⁹ Therefore its name is called Babel, because there the Lord confused the language of all the Earth; and from there the Lord scattered them abroad over the face of all the Earth. NKJV.*

However, this was corrected again by God when he reconciled humanity to himself, but on different terms. Now the languages remain different but the ability to learn and speak to them was given back to mankind on the day of Pentecost. Even today the confusion of languages remains an issue, although humanity could learn and speak each other's languages Humans cannot easily undertake projects together without disagreement, as it had happened during the building of the tower of Babel. The ability to supernaturally understand and hear the languages of various people was evidently seen during the day of the Pentecost, when different people gathered around the disciples who were waiting the coming of the Holy Spirit. Indeed, when the Holy Spirit descended upon the disciples and other people who were around them, men and women of different tribes were able to understand each other's language, indicating that they were one people with one creator-who is God. It was the final restoration of humanity back to God. God became their God again after the correction of the rebellion. The rebellion was corrected by the crucifixion of Jesus Christ on the cross. The blood and flesh of our Lord Jesus Christ restored the relationship between mankind and God.

Acts 2: ¹ When the Day of Pentecost had fully come, they were all with one accord in one place. ² And suddenly there came a sound from heaven, as of a rushing mighty wind, and it filled the whole house where they were sitting. ³ Then there appeared to them divided tongues, as of fire, and one sat upon each of them. ⁴ And they were all filled with the Holy Spirit and began to speak with other tongues, as the Spirit gave them utterance.⁵ And there were dwelling in Jerusalem Jews, devout men, from every nation under heaven. ⁶ And when this sound occurred, the multitude came together, and were confused, because everyone heard the speak in his own language. ⁷ Then they were all amazed and marvelled, saying to one another, "Look, are not all these who speak Galileans? ⁸ And how is it that we hear, each in our own language in which we were born? ⁹ Parthians and Medes and Elamites, those dwelling in Mesopotamia, Judea and Cappadocia, Pontus and Asia, ¹⁰ Phrygia and Pamphylia, Egypt and the parts of Libya adjoining Cyrene, visitors from Rome, both Jews and proselytes, ¹¹ Cretans and Arabs--we hear them speaking in our own tongues the wonderful works of God.» ¹² So they were all amazed and perplexed, saying to one another, «Whatever could this mean?» ¹³ Others mocking said, «They are full of new wine.» NKJV.

The Spirit of God, the Holy Spirit, was permanently reassigned to humanity to dwell and live in them so long as Earth remains. It is with the help of the Holy Spirit that missionaries can spread the word of God to various Peoples of the Earth today.

The second gift of the Holy Spirit is to speak the language of angels. This is a supernatural language of heaven, which no person on Earth will understand, except the one speaking it. At times the one speaking it may not even understand it. However, because of its complications and its misrepresentation by many people, it must remain a private conversation between you and God. It is recommended that this language be spoken during private prayers, dancing, and singing of hymns to God. Unless the Spirit instructs you to speak it publicly, it must remain private between one individual and his or her God. The Holy Spirit will let you speak it during your prayers if you do not know how to pray in the will of God. If we have met the right conditions for our prayers to be answered by God, the Holy Spirit takes over our prayers and intercedes for us, by directing our prayers to the will of God.

INTERPRETATION OF TONGUES

Whether in spiritual or the natural Earthly context, interpretation of tongues is needed. Sometimes the same person may be gifted both to speak and interpret the tongue or any other person who could interpret the tongues may be needed. Otherwise, there will be no reason to speak in tongues. St Paul has warned us not to speak in tongues in public or in Church when no one will understand it.

1 Corinthians 14:13-14,27-28 Therefore let him who speaks in a tongue pray that he may interpret. For if I pray in a tongue, my spirit prays, but my understanding is unfruitful. If anyone speaks in a tongue, let there be two or at the most three, each in turn, and let one interpret. But if there is no interpreter, let him keep silent in church, and let him speak to himself and to God. NKJV.

The first part of the above verses state that the Holy Spirit will help us understand what we are speaking when we speak in tongues during our prayers. The second part of the above verses states that there must be at least three people who must be present in the Church service to interpret the tongues according to their own understanding of the tongues. That is how serious God is about the interpretation of the tongues.

The interpretation of the tongues has never been without controversy. Over years, it has been used by false teachers and false prophets who speak it to deceive people. False prophets attempt to persuade people into believing that they are speaking to the angels or spirits on the behalf of the victim to bait them into a trap of deception. Obviously when people who are struggling in life with diseases, race, poverty, wars, hatred, unemployment, bareness, family violence, adultery, pornography, crimes, drug abuse and rejection, are promised deliverance from their horrific conditions, they can easily be persuaded to give-in into the deception. I have heard funny but shocking stories of which a false prophet spoke in his own mother tongue, claiming to be speaking a supernatural tongue of angels, deceive his followers into giving him money. He had done it over years to collect for himself riches, until his country natives revealed the secret to his followers that he was using his own mother tongue and not the tongue of angels to deceive his foreign victims. It was already too late by the time it was discovered, he had already bought for himself expensive cars, mansions, and a personal jet.

On the other hand, there are false prophets who speak the language of the fallen angels-headed by Satan. There are many examples in the Bible where this has occurred. A story is told in the book of **Acts 16:16, of a young girl who was used by her fortune-tellers to give them riches**. The people in Caesarea

Philippi were convinced that this young girl was being used by the spirits to accurately tell them their conditions or problems. Most people in the town were convinced by her ability to foretell their future, to the extent that when Paul and Silas cast the demonic Spirit out of her, the whole city turned against them and beat them and dragged them to the local magistrates' court to be imprisoned. The young girl had accurately identified Paul and Silas as servants of the highest God. Nevertheless, Paul and Silas got annoyed by the identification by the young girl because there was a risk of an association that could have resulted, yet they were using a different spirit to bring people to God. The purpose of the spirit of divination was to make an association with the man of God, to later convinced the people after Paul and Silas have left that there is no need to leave their demonic filled young girl for the spirit of God (Holy Spirit).

The same demonic spirit of divination is still being used today by many false prophets to deceive people, who are desperate for their healing. Although Satan and his angels are not prophetic in nature, they can accurately still have access to your past and your present to predict your future. That is all they know about you. They cannot have access fully to your future because they are no longer part of God's Kingdom. It is only God who knows what is in your future because he created you and everything you are to do on Earth. Using the Spirit of Divination, demons can attempt to have access to your future and at your present, by retrieving your records of the past, to deceptively attempt to address your current problems. Sometimes this may be true, or it may not be true, based on the person using the Spirit of Divination. A witch can entice you by telling you certain information about yourself before you even tell them, such as your address, your name, and some of your family members' names. Just to get you into deception. You will believe him or her, if they can get the information about you accurately without you telling them. At times when the Witch/Magician doesn't have your past or present information, they can use general knowledge of the situation you are going through by comparing it with other previous cases, asking you to narrate your history to them. Once you have narrated to them your problems, they will begin to provide the solution to it. Once they have promised to solve your problems they will ask to pay for the solution. But watch this; firstly, they will make sure that the problem is immediately solved so you can continue to believe in them. Secondly once the first problem is solved, they will cause more problems so that you can continue to come to them for the solution. They make sure that you are locked in permanently so that they can continue to drain your resources. If this happens to be you doing this, then you must stop immediately. The devil will never solve your problems because he is your enemy. The business of Satan is to dominate humans and destroy them. By legally joining Satan, you have joined the force for destruction. He will either cause you more problems or he will get you to cause more problems to other people. The Bible is very clear on his business in **John 10:10 *The thief comes only to steal and kill and destroy.***

4

THE FRUITS OF THE HOLY SPIRIT IN YOU

LOVE

If anything, then the entire Kingdom of God is based in love. The foundation of Christian faith is love. Inherent in every human being, is the expectation to love and to be loved back. Sometimes human beings' definition and expectation of love is totally different from God's definition and expectation of love. Perhaps people sometimes love others based on their own motivation. For example, people will love each other based on things such as money, power, relationship, knowledge, wisdom, job, education, and family background. Once the person does not meet their template of love according to these benefits, they cease to love. This love is not love at all. Let us now see the definition of love according to the Bible.

God's love is a pure love that is based on no expectations. There is no qualification for the love of God. God does not base his love on riches, beauty, money, power, relationship, or family background. He purely loves all people regardless of their condition and their situation. In fact, this love is shown by his gift to mankind – his son Jesus Christ. He gave his only begotten son to redeem humans from the law of death and sins, and Satan. Undoubtedly, humans had no ability to set themselves free from the above-mentioned punishments. So, God's love for human beings is pure and genuine.

John 3:16 For God so loved the world that He gave His only begotten Son, that whoever believes in Him should not perish but have everlasting life. NKJV.

However, this love is dependent upon who believe in him and his love for them that they should not perish. Regardless of their colour, gender, sex, race, origin, traditions, country, or continent, God's love is for everyone who believes in him. What God has not done though is to enforce his love on anyone who rejects it. That is why people continue to go to hell even though they have been set free from permanent isolation of sins against God. God's love is uniquely amazing in that he even continues to love his enemies. He continues to send his sun, rain, air, and all seasons on both good and evil people on Earth. This is the love God wants from his children.

God wants his children to love people unconditionally just as he does. We must not love people in return of what they can do for us or expectations. Despite people's financial, social, political, and spiritual affiliations, he wants us to love anyway. Just like God, we must not love for our own benefits. Whether people love us or hate us we must continue to love them without prejudices or expectations. God wants us to even love our enemies. There is no benefit in loving those who love us, because that is a common practice by those who do not know God. What is the point of being like them? If we love because we expect to be loved back or for material resources, then that is not love but an act of expectations and submission. We are expected to love our enemies; those who curse us, those who hate us and those who spitefully use us and persecute us. The best example of this love is what our Lord Jesus Christ showed on the cross when he was being crucified, and said, "Father, forgive them, for they do not know what they do (Luke 23:34)." People who betrayed and crucified Jesus Christ never knew that they were being freed from their own death caused by their own sins. He died on the cross on their behalf because of his love for them in order to set them free from the spirit of death, with which Satan had power to kill them. Yes, indeed they never knew what they were doing; had they known they would have not crucified him on the cross, because Jesus' death was for their own good. God left heaven because of this pure love and came to the Earth, to set humanity free from the dominance of the spirit of death, and Satan who had power over humans. Christ came to suffer shame, humiliation, and death on behalf of mankind because of his love for them.

Therefore, as Christians we are expected to replicate to others what Christ did on the cross for us. We are expected to know better the consequences of sins and death, in order to win people to God. Permanent isolation from God is something you would want your fellow human being to avoid. What would be the point of expecting to go to a beautiful place free of torment (heaven) and expect your brother or sister to end up in hell, a place of permanent torment. Besides that, as Christians we have no enemies if are born-again, unless we are deceiving ourselves. We do not have enemies because of God's protection and his love for us. No Devil can curse what God has blessed. So, we do not have enemies including Satan himself, if we are born-again. Those people who think they are our enemies are not our enemies because they lack the knowledge we have in God. Instead, having this knowledge in God we must overcome their enmity by winning them over to Christ by doing good to them. In order for your enemy to know the good part of you, you must do good to them, and you will win them over to your side.

Likewise, as God has individually loved us, we must also individually love others. God through love has individually forgiven, each of our sins. No matter what sin you have committed, God has forgiven you. Hence, because of this we must also unconditionally forgive those people who have sinned against us. Just as God has forgiven us without any conditions. The true definition of love is to be unselfish, self-denying, and have affection for someone else's needs and concerns above our own. Often people find it so difficult to love selfish and wretched people. It is sometimes understandable why it may be difficult if people do not appreciate what we have done for them. But that is why we have the Holy Spirit, who can give us comfort when we are dealing with unappreciative people. That is why love is a fruit of the Holy Spirit. When we find it very difficult to love others, we should consult with the Holy Spirit, who will give us the ability to love others. You can be a great man or woman of God but if you do not love people, you will achieve nothing in your walk with God. Without humility and love for others you will have no ground to succeed in the work of God. In fact, God is love and we must also act in love. If you claim to love God and hate your fellow humans, then you are deceiving yourself.

JOY

Joy is the complete inner happiness, delight, and gladness of one's heart. What have you noticed so far? Everything we are talking about here is spiritual in nature, including joy. The only way you can enjoy the Kingdom of God is to focus on your inner peace. You cannot experience these things physically unless you have first experienced them spiritually. When there is inner joy in a person it can be experienced physically in the form of a smile, singing, dancing, and laughers. That is why you can meet a person and you can tell from their physical look without speaking to them that he or she has joy or has no joy in life. In this world it is very difficult to experience and maintain continuous joy daily due to bad news that confronts us every day, such as the death of our loved ones, wars, hunger, loss of job, demotion, violence, financial crisis, collapse of business, bitter divorce, accident and so forth. This is because we live in a broken world of tribulation, distress, persecution, famine, sword and peril. It is a broken world, and we must accept that it is. We must be physically and mentally prepared for any eventuality always. That is why we must be in the lord in order to overcome them. For some people, it seems nothing can keep them happy, and when they are happy it will always be short-lived. This is the mentality of some people. That is why they hunt to seek out joy in the things of this world.

For example, people of this world attempt to seek out joy in things such as a nice family, car, house, money, power, clothes, friends, education, and tourism and even in the worse-case scenario, seeking after demonic powers to solve their problems. But all these things are in vain without God. The true joy that will last comes from God. There is nothing among these things plus other things I have not mentioned here, that can bring you joy. In as much as these things are good, they cannot be used in exchange for joy. These things are of the physical dimension, whereas joy is in the spiritual dimension. That is why many people are disappointed after having acquired all these things, because of the lack of joy in them. There will always be a spiritual loophole in your life unless you are seeking after the things of the Spirit. You can obtain God's joy if you have knowledge of the source of true joy. You will only have joy when you have the Spirit of God working actively within.

Romans 14:17 For the kingdom of God is not eating and drinking, but righteousness and peace and joy in the Holy Spirit. 18 For he who serves Christ in these things is acceptable to God and approved by men. NKJV.

We have these problems which will keep us away from experiencing our joy because of our human heart. The human heart is the most wicked thing above all else, and unless you allow God to change it, it shall remain doomed. Where do you think hatred, jealousy, rebellion, murder, selfishness, anger, violence, covetousness, stealing, corruption, greed and so more come from? They come from the human heart. If you want to change a person, then you must change their heart. It is only God who can do it. The only way out of all of these sins is our Lord Jesus Christ. He said, In the world you will have troubles but be cheerful – I have overcome the world (John 16:33). Christ is the solution to the problems of all humanity.

Additionally, as a Christian you will have trouble because of your faith in God and your assignment from God that will sometimes steal your joy away because of the resistance by demonic powers. No one becomes a born-again Christian without discovering new ways of doing things in the Christian faith. One of those things is constant prayer. Christians are exhorted to pray continuously without ceasing if they are to win against demonic powers. When you become a born-again Christian with the Holy Spirit actively working in your life, you become a threat to the demonic powers ruling the world, and prayer is no longer an option for you but a lifestyle, if you are to win against the Satanic powers. If God begins to reveal to you the real threat posed to you by the demonic powers, you will be constantly seeking God for protection, direction, and wisdom on how to operate in this dangerous world.

Besides these problems we must trust and believe that God is in control no matter what we go through or what happens to us in this life. God created everything and he is in control of everything. In fact, the presence of the Holy Spirit within us, brings us continuous daily joy if we allow him to lead us. We are encouraged to rejoice in the Lord, not in the things of this world. Even as we go through difficulties, God will continue to bring us continuous joy to overcome every problem we experience in this life. We must be excited in what we do in life, whether it is from God or our fellow human beings. Everything that we do to bring joy to people is what we must continue to do. The great example of joyous moments of St Paul were in the book of **Philippians 4:1 *Therefore, my beloved and longed-for brethren, my joy and crown, stand fast in the Lord, beloved.*** As a gospel preacher, he was pleased with how the Philippian Christians had received his message of salvation. This was manifested in the way they loved God, their fellow brethren, their generosity towards the gospel preachers, and their physical and spiritual health and prosperity in the things of God. They were his joy because they had understood and applied the word of God in their lives. There is nothing that can bring you joy more than what you do to change peoples' lives for the better.

St Paul urged us to not just have fleeting moments of joy, but to continue to rejoice always in the Lord (Philippians 4:4). What does this mean in context? It means that if we are to have constant joyous moments in life, then God should be the source of our joy. Every time we get disappointed with issues of life then we must run back to God to seek his, guidance, direction and solution that will bring us happiness and joy. There is no problem God cannot fix. What do you think will happen to us when we have our difficult problems fixed? We will always be happy and joyful. He also argued us to maintain our joy when we have it.

We must not forget that joy is a fruit of Holy Spirit, and the way to maintain it is to maintain the presence of the Holy Spirit. The only way you can maintain the presence of the Holy Spirit is to have a clear mind that focuses on the things of God. The Spirit of God will never be present in an environment where people are abusive, unkind, envious, jealous, violent, and aggressive. Hence, St Paul said that you must pay attention to those things that are joyful; **Philippians 4:8** *Finally, brethren, whatever things are true, whatever things are noble, whatever things are just, whatever things are pure, whatever things are lovely, whatever things are of good report, if there is any virtue and if there is anything praiseworthy--meditate on these things. ⁹ The things which you learned and received and heard and saw in me, these do, and the God of peace will be with you.* **NKJV.**

PEACE

All things work together for good to those who love God, (Romans 8:28). This statement is the statement of peace itself. Whether good or bad, if all things can work together for, we who love God, then we have peace of mind over those things that are troubling us. The peace of God which surpasses all understanding is what you need in the time of trouble as a Christian. Peace of God means a total calmness and quietness of our souls and spirits during the storms of our lives. The presence of God within us gives us exercises of faith in him and what he says in his word. The peace of God which surpasses all understanding is given to us by God. It is the presence of God in our lives, as the controller of all things. No matter the circumstance we are going through, whether it is death, ridicule, torture, shipwreck, toil, or other forms of persecution, our peace in God must not be shaken. I will start with these favourite verses in the Bible;

Philippians 4:6 Be anxious for nothing, but in everything by prayer and supplication, with thanksgiving, let your requests be made known to God; 7 and the peace of God, which surpasses all understanding, will guard your hearts and minds through Christ Jesus. NKJV.

In the above two verses St Paul has stated very clearly that firstly, we must not be worried over everything bad that comes our way, but instead bow down in prayer, asking God to solve it for us. While we ask him in prayer, we must be certain that we are heard, and God will solve our problems. The reason we thank him is the fact that nothing is impossible with him, and whatever we ask him through prayer, he will bring to pass, so long as we have made it known to him. Secondly, this is a beautiful and encouraging part; the peace of God will take care of our spirit and soul, that are badly affected by any difficult situation we face. Our spirit and soul are the most affected parts of us because they are spiritual. Therefore, almost all the problems we go through in this life have the spiritual dimensions that we must pay attention to.

Again, peace is spiritual in nature, and we can feel it in our innermost being. Before the peace can be seen outwardly it can be first felt inwardly by your spirit and your soul. I cannot emphasise this enough; your spirit and soul are the true you. Your spirit and soul cannot be satisfied by the physical things or the material things of the world. People can have the physical things of this world and still lack peace. You can have your education, job, family, power, business, mansions, cars, and private jet and still have no peace. These things will never give you peace. And if they do give you peace then it may be short-lived.

The presence of God within us in the form of the Holy Spirit gives us complete peace. A peace that surpasses human understanding. It is a peace that despite the circumstances you are facing, you will remain standing, and people will be wondering why you are still standing. This peace comes with the confidence that God is in control of all things including the problems we are facing. It is knowing the character of God that he is faithful and just, and that he will not allow you to be tempted beyond what you are able to stand but will give you a way to escape. We must keep things in perspective when we develop a close relationship with God, that there is nothing which is impossible with him. Undoubtedly, he is the Lord of all things and the Lord over all things.

Peace becomes a weapon of war if God is with us. For example, Jesus Christ appeared to the frightened disciples in their hiding place because of their fear of Jews and said to them; "Peace be with you (John 20:19)." As they were being hunted down because of their association with Jesus, fear became a weapon of the Jews, against them. Exactly in the same way when Jesus appeared to them in the hiding room, peace became a weapon, as they had a sense of relief with his presence. Immediately as they saw the Lord, fear lifted, and they were all glad about the presence of God in their midst. Having peace, they were commissioned to go to the world and preach the gospel. He breathed on them the Holy Spirit, who was instrumental in their work on Earth. They had to be guided by the Holy Spirit in order to preach the gospel and to maintain their peace.

John 20: [19] Then, the same day at evening, being the first day of the week, when the doors were shut where the disciples were assembled, for fear of the Jews, Jesus came and stood in the midst, and said to them, «Peace be with you.» [20] When He had said this, He showed them His hands and His side. Then the disciples were glad when they saw the Lord. [21] So Jesus said to them again, «Peace to you! As the Father has sent Me, I also send you.» [22] And when He had said this, He breathed on them, and said to them, "Receive the Holy Spirit. [23] If you forgive the sins of any, they are forgiven them; if you retain the sins of any, they are retained." NKJV.

LONGSUFFERING

Sometimes we suffer because of our own making or sometimes when God allow it to happen to us. Either way God will turn it for good even if it is our own fault, when we run to him for the solution, and if it is he who has allowed us to go through the suffering, then he will be right with us to see it through. God will sometimes allow us to go through problems for our own good. In trouble we are trained to be perfect. God tests us for our good and Satan tempts us for our downfall. There is not any single person in the world or in the Bible who has not gone through difficulty in order to becomes great. In other words, things we go through in this life are there to be managed by us, but not to manage us. No one can become great without overcoming difficult situations. With this argument so far, your head may be spinning, as to whether I am encouraging you to celebrate problems. No. I am not celebrating problems, neither do I want you to go through problems, however, when problems come against you, you must be able to solve them. We must receive problems with the confidence to solve them.

If we are to be successful Christians in our God-called life, then we must have these three important words at our figure tips and apply them in every situation: patience, endurance, and perseverance. All these words sound like they have the same meaning, but they are totally different. According to the Cambridge dictionary: patience is the ability to wait, or to continue doing something despite difficulties, or to suffer without complaining or becoming annoyed; endurance is the ability to keep doing something difficult, unpleasant, or painful for a long time. Whereas perseverance is continued effort to do or achieve something, even when this is difficult or takes a long time. You can see how these words are totally different in their meaning, but you still need them both in every difficult situation you may find yourself in. Patience in every difficult situation will save us time, energy and resources that could have been wasted had we been impatient. We need patience in meetings, arguments, shopping centres, on roads, hotels and more importantly with our family members. We live today in a highly pressurised society where no one wants to wait a little bit. For example, many people have been killed or injured on the roads due to road rage, which could have been avoided had one of the parties involved been patient and given in to the other impatient person. It doesn't kill to wait. It just takes a few seconds for things to be out of control if we are not patient. Moreover, endurance is a key ingredient of our Christian faith. When we endure for a very long time in a difficult situation and do not give up, we are most likely to win. In fact, endurance will be so important during these difficult end times. People will be persecuted for their faith in God and many people's faith will grow cold as a result. But our Lord Jesus Christ said, they that will endure to the end will be saved. If endurance can then bring us salvation, then you must not take it lightly. Perseverance will give us new character and form a completely a new person in us if we are consistent enough to overcome the situation. If you know the end goal of what you want, then you must learn to persevere to achieve it. If we know what we want, then we must not worry too much about how long it may take to get it.

Undoubtedly God allows us to go through very difficult situations for our good. The potential to overcome that situation is always within us. God will never allow you to go through a difficult situation, if he knows you cannot manage. Unless you brought the problems on yourself due to your bad decisions, God will make sure he sees you through. But even if it was your fault and you repent and run to him, he will still see you through. Pay attention to what he wants to do through you. But even if you had brought the problems on yourself, he would also fix it if you ran back to him and acknowledged your sin before him. God is not a son of man to reject people because of their mistakes nor does he laugh at us when we go through the problems of our own making. Run to him if you have a problem you are experiencing, and you do not know how to fix it or you do not have a way out. The book of Romans is very clear on this.

Romans 5: ³ And not only that, but we also glory in tribulations, knowing that tribulation produces perseverance; ⁴ and perseverance, character; and character, hope. ⁵ Now hope does not disappoint, because the love of God has been poured out in our hearts by the Holy Spirit who was given to us. NKJV.

St Paul is telling us here that we must be happy when we go through suffering or tribulations knowing that they will produce perseverance. Perseverance in turn will build new character in us that will bring us hope. A new character built in us, will give us skills, abilities, strength, knowledge, and ways of doing things that will give us hope that does not disappoint. By this you can rediscover powerful parts of you that were hidden before the problems came your way. Once you have hope then I can absolutely tell you that hope cannot fail you. The reason why the hope cannot fail you is because it is a responsibility of the Spirit of God to bring to pass the solution needed for your problems. You know that if God oversees your problems, then nothing will stop him from bringing your solution to pass, whatever you are waiting on him for, because there is nothing impossible with him.

Long suffering is one of the fruits of the Holy Spirit that is needed by the Christian. Think about this; if God had to strike down people every time, they made a mistake, no one would live. He has every weapon at disposal to judge and to destroy, but at the same he has the character of being our father and he will not kill his children whenever they make mistakes. Instead, he is patient, until they realise their mistake and turn away from it. The Holy Spirit wants to impart the same character into us if we are born-again Christians. While we discharge our Christian duties, we must be patient with all people, hoping that if they wrong us or commit mistakes while carrying out their duties, we must be patient and be willing to forgive them. The Holy Spirit will be willing to teach us patience in everything we do by making sure that our emotions, thoughts, imaginations, and character are up to the task.

God allows us sometimes to go through suffering in order not to trust in ourselves and our solutions for the problem. God is after his glory and everyone that goes through suffering, if set free, must not claim credit for the breakthrough. It is very common today in the world not to give God credit for the accident we survived, the sickness we are healed from, gun-shot wounds we survived, natural disasters that missed us including our own homes being spared, and even deadly wars we have survived. It is important to give God credit and glory for the things we survive which are beyond our control, and which would have turned into a disaster without his invisible intervention. Let us see what St Paul says about suffering in the book of.

2 Corinthians 1:3 Blessed be the God and Father of our Lord Jesus Christ, the Father of mercies and God of all comfort, [4] who comforts us in all our tribulation, that we may be able to comfort those who are in any trouble, with the comfort with which we ourselves are comforted by God. ⁵ For as the sufferings of Christ abound in us, so our consolation also abounds through Christ. ⁶ Now if we are afflicted, it is for your consolation and salvation, which is effective for enduring the same sufferings which we also suffer. Or if we are comforted, it is for your consolation and salvation.⁷ And our hope for you is steadfast, because we know that as you are partakers of the sufferings, so also you will partake of the consolation. ⁸ For we do not want you to be ignorant, brethren, of our trouble which came to us in Asia: that we were burdened beyond measure, above strength, so that we despaired even of life. ⁹ Yes, we had the sentence of death in ourselves, that we should not trust in ourselves but in God who raises the dead, ¹⁰ who delivered us from so great a death, and does deliver us; in whom we trust that He will still deliver us, ¹¹ you also helping together in prayer for us, that thanks may be given by many persons on our behalf for the gift granted to us through many. NKJV.

St Paul says here that firstly, we go through suffering in order to comfort our other fellow human beings who may go through the same suffering in the future. Secondly, it is a good thing to suffer for your salvation because it is the only way you can have it. Once you become a born-again Christian, the enemy of your soul, Satan will come after you. He came from heaven, and he does not want anyone to go to heaven. Because he is envious of you. He knows how beautiful heaven is and he will never go there forever and so he is not happy about your salvation. But not only that, he is not happy with you because of the number of people you teach about Christ. Any assignment from God meets resistance from Satan because he wants to be worshipped. In fact, that is why he rebelled against God in the first place – for worship. He would rather want you to worship places, people, water, rivers, shrines, mountains, animals, plants, sun, moon, and stars, than to worship God. Thirdly, it is an opportunity for us to pray for each other as Christians if we are going through challenges. Whatever we have overcome is what we are assured of another victory tomorrow. When we have gone through attacks and prayed for each other, we will be better placed tomorrow to defeat similar attacks, if they come our way, through prayer. A soldier that has gone to war and the soldier that has not gone to war are totally different. The one who has gone to war is much better positioned to defeat the enemy in the future because he has had experience of war. It is a similar scenario with Christians; the more they defeat the enemy through prayer, the more they are likely to defeat the enemy of their souls through the same prayers tomorrow. God is victor and must be victorious too. He has put all his enemies under his feet on the cross. The victory is yours. Fight the good fight of faith and you will be victorious. Nothing is new under the sun; what you are going through, someone else has gone through before you. If it's too hard for you, God will not allow you to go through it. But not only that, he is there with you in your suffering, just learn to hear him.

KINDNESS

We live in what almost everyone calls a dangerous world today because most people have rejected Christian values including kindness. We have refused to treat other people the way we ourselves would love to be treated. Whether good or bad, what we do to others must be also be reciprocally done to us. What we expect of others must also be expected of us by others. Nothing works mysteriously without our involvement.

There is a real challenge in contemporary society to be kind to those who do not accept your beliefs and your stand on certain agendas. We must be able to reach people without letting our core beliefs be eroded by those who are not kind to us, in order not to be hurt by their unbelief and inaction. The only way we can reach out to people is to be grounded in the word of God, gifts, and the fruits of the Holy Spirit. We must build our house on the rock and not the sand. For example, many Christians today find it very difficult to reach out and be kind to the gay and lesbian community based on their contrary beliefs to Christian beliefs. We can still be kind to them as God's creation and as people, even though we do not agree with their beliefs. We are all sinners and what we can do is to bring them to Christ for their beliefs to be changed. Christ is the answer to all sins. He came to save all sinners including ourselves and them. What we must not do though is to accept their sin as normal and be part of their beliefs.

God himself commanded us to love each other. A commandment is an order to be done. We have a responsibility to be kind to each other without sharing the same beliefs. God wants us, his children, to be kind to others even though we know them as our enemies. When we do good to them, our actions will communicate to them louder than our words, which can hurt them. We can easily overcome their fear and their unbelief of us with our actions towards them. It is by doing so that we can overcome the evil with good. For example, if you go to the beach and see someone drowning in the ocean, the first impression that comes into your mind is to stop them from, drowning despite what they might believe in. The reason you would act this way is the fact that you do not want your fellow human being to die on your watch. The person you have helped or rescued in return will appreciate your actions and may be friends with you forever. Sometimes it takes our simple action to change a person for life.

Ephesians 4: 25 Therefore, putting away lying, "Let each one of you speak truth with his neighbour," for we are members of one another. 26 "Be angry, and do not sin": do not let the sun go down on your wrath, 27 nor give place to the devil. 28 Let him who stole steal no longer, but rather let him labour, working with his hands what is good, that he may have something to give him who has need. 29 Let no corrupt word proceed out of your mouth, but what is good for necessary edification, that it may impart grace to the hearers. NKJV.

When we act with kindness towards others it brings harmony to human society. The reason we have a chaotic world today is that no one wants to be kind. No one wants to be patient a little bit and say sorry to the person they have wronged or who has wronged them. Everyone must see everything in their own eyes as right and not wrong. No one wants to admit their mistakes. No one wants to be seen as a coward after they are wronged. We are all obliged to pay back in the same way. We seem to embrace this saying, "An eye for an eye, makes the whole world blind." There are people, no matter what we do to them, who remain unreceptive to our kindness. These are people who have deep wounds of bitterness, anger, and resentment towards other people. If you meet such people, you must avoid them at all costs. They are too negative and driven by confrontations. They cannot rest until they have caused problems. It is okay to disagree, but it must be done respectfully. Imagine our Lord Jesus Christ avoiding the entire hometown of Galilee because of their unbelief. People continue to go to hell today not because they have not heard the gospel message but because of their ignorance of it.

Having the mind-set of kindness always will help people who are struggling in life and who may need your particular words at that given moment in time. You may be passing by a person who is about to commit suicide or who is depressed and your kind words to them may help them at that moment. This was exactly what our Lord was doing when he was here on Earth, every time he was moving about and saw a crowd that needed healing, he was always moved with compassion to healed all. Every time he was moving on the road for a different mission and heard people calling out loud to him for healing, he stopped and healed them. Whether inside our home or out on the road we must be willing to listen to people's concerns and where possible, accord our help. Our kind words can heal broken hearted people at any given moment in time. For example, think about those people who spoke to you at your darkest moments in life. When you never knew whether you would make it in life. Those kind words lifted your spirit up and got you going in life. Our words can build us up or can tear us down as human beings.

Kindness is fruit of the Holy Spirit. Once the Holy Spirit is in you it becomes very easy to be kind to other people. Kindness goes hand in hand with love. You can always be kind to your loved ones. Remember to do to others what you want to be done to you. Be kind, be gentle, be hospitable to other human beings and you will receive the same from them and for that matter from God.

GOODNESS

Goodness is the selfless act towards others. It is beneficence to others. It is the ability to do good to others without expectations of return or pay back. A good person does not manipulate, intimidate or dominate others to his or her advantage. They do things out of a pure heart to others in love. Once these kinds of people are noticed by others, they become trustworthy and reliable to them. This is expected by the non-believers and believers alike from every believer in God. It is very common among non-Christians to believe that all Christians are good. It is always a surprise to non-believers when a Christian commits sin. There is nothing wrong at all in expecting Christians to exhibit goodness because they are the representatives of God on Earth. But it is not non-Christians alone who expect Christians to be good, but also our Lord Jesus Christ, wants them to show goodness, and be an example to others by doing good. Christians are asked by our Lord Jesus Christ to fight evil with good and not to be tired of doing good to others. The only way we can become the true salt of Earth is to lead by example in doing good to others. Christians are the exemplar of the world for study by non-believers. If we are to win people over to Christ, those who follow Christ must always do good and show goodness to others. There are many stories of non-Christians being saved through the good works of Christians. Even if a non-believer had no intention to believe in God, the goodness of the Christian towards them can draw them to God.

Goodness is an important fruit of the Holy Spirit, that is planted in the anointed believer. It is always very hard for a believer who has the anointing of the Holy Spirit not to show and be a good example of goodness to others. You can easily tell those who have this fruit of the Holy Spirit deep inside, through their words and actions. These people are good to the core of their character and personality. When this personality of the Holy Spirit is deeply ingrained in them, there is an immediate attraction of other people towards them. The goodness of the living God who draws people to him, can also draw people to us when we have the Holy Spirit operating within us.

The true Christian with the fruit of goodness in him or her has nothing to fear. God wants us to be role models of goodness, when we have the Holy Spirit operating within. This should be good news to every Christian, that if we have God within us then we do not have enemies. And if we do have enemies then we should easily defeat them because we have a powerful God, who cannot be defeated. In addition, he has already defeated our enemies on our behalf and therefore we have nothing to fear. We must always live from the position of victory of God no matter what comes our way. No Satanic powers can defeat us whether it is witchcraft, sorcery, or divination. No one can curse what God blessed and no one can bless what God has cursed. No other people are as free on Earth as the children of God, because they live in the unshakeable kingdom. That is why God wants us to pray, do good and bless those who persecute, oppress, curse and spitefully use us. They do this in ignorance of the fact that we cannot be defeated.

We can pray that God will have mercy for these people that they might have eternal life, that we are sure to enjoy, in the afterlife. If you know your brother or sister is going into the fire, you will do everything in your power to save them. You will never wish them bad if you know the consequences of getting burned by fire. This is exactly what God wants us to do for the non-believers for them to have life. Because we know that without Christ there is no life.

FAITHFULNESS

Faithfulness is a quality or an act of being loyal, reliable, and trustworthy to both God and people. This quality is defined in Bible dictionary as a state of a person having fidelity which makes them true to their promise and faithful to their task. Fidelity makes them steadfast, dedicated, dependable and worthy of trust. Fidelity keeps us steadfast, unchanging, and thoroughly grounded in relation to the other. And fidelity brings dependability, loyalty, and stability. In this broken world, it is very hard to find a faithful person, without their hidden interests. It is also very hard for others to trust us. Hence, if we cannot be trusted by others then we might also find it hard to trust others. However, there are still some people who can trust us and whom we can also trust. At times they may be Christians. Some of them have given their lives and their ways to God, and as a result find it difficult to cheat, and some of them may not be Christians but they are mindful of their reputations to others, that they are not wrongly perceived.

Faithfulness is an important character of God. He is faithful to himself and to mankind. That is why what he says must happen – will happen. This is why we can trust him. He promised, and he keeps his promises because no one else is above him. Imagine if God was never faithful to his words; everything in Heaven and on Earth would be in disorder. As Christians we have a responsibility to adopt this character of God which is trustworthy to both God and men. God does not want to work with a person he cannot trust, neither do humans want to do the same. It is one thing to believe in God, but it is another to be faithful to him. This is what sometimes affects our relationship with him. If we try to hide some of our information, thoughts, words, and actions from him, even though he knows them, then we are not trustworthy to him, and he cannot work with us. When we are faithful to God, he will build in us a new character that is not only trustworthy to him but to others. If God builds a new character within us, then we can also be trusted by our fellow human beings. It is certain that if we can be trusted by God then we can be trusted by people. This relationship cannot be driven by the knowledge that if God or others are watching over us then we must behave differently. Our actions must be driven by the knowledge that whether God is watching us in secret or others are watching us in person, we must always do the right thing. We must not be governed by rules and regulations of other people to do the right thing. This how you can be called a trustworthy human being. For example, Abraham developed his trust of God and vice versa. God developed his trust in Abraham, and despite the number of years that passed, God had to finally bless Abraham with his son of promise.

    We grow in faithfulness through our relationship with the Holy Spirit, who is faithful to us. Even though we are unfaithful and doubt God's faithfulness, he still does what he wants to do through us. It may take a long time to build this character in us but if we are committed to his teachings, we can eventually be changed to the person God wants us to be. The mistake we may make is to give up the training of the Holy Spirit. We suffer because of this training, but we must continue to commit to the character of God. Knowing that he is faithful, and he has no intention to destroy us but to train us for our good. The training may seem difficult, but we will eventually enjoy its fruits if our training is successful. We had better commit ourselves to this training so that we may live the rest of our lives sinlessly. The more we train to understand the consequences of sins, the less likely we are to commit one.

Hebrews 12:10 For they indeed for a few days chastened us as seemed best to them, but He for our profit, that we may be partakers of His holiness. 11 Now no chastening seems to be joyful for the present, but painful; nevertheless, afterward it yields the peaceable fruit of righteousness to those who have been trained by. NKJV.

1 Peter 4:1 Therefore, since Christ suffered for us in the flesh, arm yourselves also with the same mind, for he who has suffered in the flesh has ceased from sin, 2 that he no longer should live the rest of his time in the flesh for the lusts of men, but for the will of God. 3 For we have spent enough of our past lifetime in doing the will of the Gentiles--when we walked in lewdness, lusts, drunkenness, revelries, drinking parties, and abominable idolatries. NKJV.

There are three important take-aways from this faithfulness of God. Firstly, it is for our salvation. Although salvation is given to us free of charge, God does not want sin and for that matter does not want his children to live a sinful life on Earth. This is for a simple reason; God, wants his children be role models for the children of the world, to win them over to him. Secondly, for moral attributes God does not want his children to live below the standards of the world and the laws of the world. World laws are made for those stubborn and naughty unruly children of the world. We as children of God must be morally righteous and do not need anyone in the world to tell us the right things to do. Their rules and regulations, and codes of conduct may be in place to govern us, and we must do the right thing always so these rules may remain irrelevant to us. We must always be above the world standards and above world laws. If we are persecuted, we must be persecuted doing the right things for God who will intervene on our behalf. While we are innocent, God can quickly intervene on our behalf. He loves when we are persecuted for nothing so that he can show off his power to the children of the wicked. Thirdly, we are the light and the salt of the Earth. We are only distinguished as children of light by what we do differently from the world. We must represent God's Kingdom on Earth in the right ways. We are copied by the world. Nothing makes the living God prouder than for his children to attract the children of the world to him. He loves it when he is praised through our actions. When he has imparted his character of faithfulness to us, he steps back and allows us to operate freely in winning people to him.

Proverbs 3:3 Let love and faithfulness never leave you; bind them around your neck, write them on the tablet of your heart 4 Then you will win favor and a good name in the sight of God and man. NIV.

GENTLENESS

Gentleness is the quality or character of being humble, compassionate, and considerate towards each other as human beings. We exercise gentleness in the way we care and love for each other through our conduct and our words. Gentleness is reflected in the way we speak and act towards each other. Having a calm spirit or nature is the true meaning of gentleness. We are considered gentle in the way we respond to situations and conditions, especially in worse-case situations. This character does not develop quickly; sometimes we must face a situation threatening our very existence. There is a strong connection between what we say and how we conduct ourselves in dire situations. What we do or what we speak when we are angry can diffuse or can fuel the situation. When we are gentle, we can easily be trusted by others. Being gentle makes others listen and do what we tell them to do.

Let me make this clear; gentleness is not weakness, although many people think it is. This perception is the reason why we lack many gentle men and women today in the world. The world is so chaotic because we are not gentle to our fellow human beings. We do not give a chance to people to explain themselves as to why they have wronged us. We are not patient enough to listen to voices of peace more than the voices of war. We are not patient enough to pursue our problem in the court of law or to allow other people to listen to our problems. Yet all we are quick to do is just to pay back evil for evil the way it has been done to us. This could be the reason among others why there is an increase in violence at all levels of our human society today. Because we have lost this important fruit of the Holy Spirit. When we lose God's knowledge on Earth, we are most likely to do what is right in our own eyes. We are all prideful in nature. Fighting among ourselves destroys our relationships and it takes a long time to restore them.

Gentleness is humility. Humility is not weakness but rather calmness, patience, and exercise of self-control in any given situation or condition. Gentleness means that a person sees the immediate problems and solves them differently. Gentle people may sometimes see themselves differently from the people who are involved with them in conflict because of the information they have about the problem. Even if they have been wronged, they put themselves and their interests below the interests of the person who has wronged them. They sometimes see the problems and the situation of other people differently and may be able to provide a different solution. A good example of this was the solution provided by our Lord Jesus Christ in the case of the adulterous woman who was brought to him to judge (John 8:3). Everyone was convinced that the woman should be stoned to death, but Christ showed his gentleness to the woman by convicting the Pharisees of their own sins. People who had gathered to stone her were all sinners and they had to leave the woman alone, while Christ did not condemn the woman, but instead forgave and asked her to go and not sin again.

When we are gentle, we will not fuel the problem further by contributing to it. Being self-willed and self-righteous make it difficult for us to be gentle to others. People who act like this are most likely to quickly judge others for their mistakes, yet they are blinded to their own mistakes. We are most likely to be gentle if we put the interests of other people above ours. If we think about others and how they will think or respond to us when we wrong them, then we are most likely to stay gentle to everyone. Think about this; what is the point of going to war and later find out that you were wrong? We are most likely to suffer the consequences of our actions if we react quickly and impatiently to them. Instead, we need to have gentleness and give second thought of our actions before we commit them. So, gentleness cannot be wrong; we must think before we act. That is true gentleness.

God is gentle and slow to anger. That is why we exist today in the world. If God had to deal with our sins the way, we deserve then there would be no single human being on this planet. Think about this; God allows his sun, moon, stars, air, water, plants, and animals to be enjoyed by sinners and particularly those who reject him and his existence. If he had to act like sons and daughters of man, he would have removed the wicked men and women already. He wants his children to be gentle like him. Because gentleness is a fruit of the Holy Spirit, it comes automatically to us if we allow the Holy Spirit to live within us. In fact, people who are gentle, meek and humble are promised by God to inherit the Earth. How do you inherit the Earth? By living long on it and thereafter your salvation comes back with Christ to live it in for one thousand years.

Matthew 5:5 Blessed are the meek, for they shall inherit the Earth. NKJV.

Revelation 20:4 And I saw thrones, and they sat on them, and judgment was committed to them. Then I saw the souls of those who had been beheaded for their witness to Jesus and for the word of God, who had not worshipped the beast or his image, and had not received his mark on their foreheads or on their hands. And they lived and reigned with Christ for a thousand years. NKJV.

Gentleness is not just good for us alone it is also good for our families and churches. So much of the peace we yearn for at home is related to how we treat each other at home. If we are to have a peaceful home, then we must be respectful to each other. The same should be equally true for the churches. We must be willing to forgive each other in the church when we have wronged each other. How is it good not to admit our mistakes in front of our fellow Christians to later admit before the non-Christians? In fact, if our yes was yes then we have no need to go to the court of pagans. As soon as we heed to Christ's call for gentleness to each other as Christians, then we will not have wars in the churches as we sometimes see today. Here are some of the ways we can show gentleness to each other; be humble when you serve others, exercise calmness during violence, act with love to others, seek and live in peace with other people, select your words and speak them carefully to others, respect other people's opinions when you disagree with them, exercise patience and show empathy in every situation that needs it, and be considerate to others people's needs and feelings. Remember to do to others that which you want done to you.

SELF-CONTROL

According to the great man of God, Michael Bradley, self-control is a state of having temperance, rational restraint of natural impulses, sobriety, calmness, a dispassionate approach to life, and mastery of personal desires and passions. It calls for restraint and a self-disciplined life following Christ's example of being in the world but not of the world.

We live in a materialistic world in which it is very hard to exercise self-control. But the fact is, if you cannot control yourself then you cannot control someone else. We are created with a fallen nature that has more propensity to sin than to act in righteousness. We are more likely to commit sin than to do good by ourselves when do not exercise self-control. If we do not have self-control our sinful nature of greed, lying, lust, jealousy, gossips, hatred, violence and so much more can easily kick in and overtake us if we are not careful. Our sinful nature will compel us to get things done quickly without a second thought. We quickly commit acts we later regret if we do not have self-control. There is nothing worse than a man and a woman who cannot control themselves.

Self-control is an important fruit of the Holy Spirit that we badly need in the world today if we are to succeed in what we do as Christians. Because it is the fruit of the Holy Spirit, if we commit ourselves to the guidance of the Holy Spirit, he can control us, particularly our words and our actions. In fact, when the Holy Spirit begins to take control of our nature, our flesh begins to war against our spirit nature. No true man or woman of God, who is born-again of the Holy Spirit can claim not to have experienced this war within themselves. Sometimes this war may even get worse, and our sinful nature begins to be disobedient to the Holy Spirit. That is why St Paul warned us not to quench or grieve the Holy Spirit. When part of us is out of control, no matter what the sin, it can bring death.

We must allow the Holy Spirit of God to sanctify us to the degree he would like if we were to have self-control in full. No matter if you think you have control over yourself, wait until you get provoked and get angry. You will see your true fallen nature that you never once thought you had. Hence, you will have no or little victory over things such as temptation, unforgiveness, fear, doubt, drunkenness, lust, greed, and judgemental and critical demonic spirits. Indeed, Satan and his demons easily defeat us because of our fallen nature that is out of control. Interestingly our fallen nature can attract demonic spirits. Before a demonic spirit comes in to enslave you there must be part of you that is out of control which may be, disobedience to parents, sexual immorality, greed, corruption, lying, gossips, love of money, pride, and all forms of fleshly pleasures.

5

THE FEAR OF GOD IN YOU

Fear of the Lord has been taken out of context on many occasions by Christians and non-Christians alike. But what does fear of the Lord really mean? What does it mean when you fear someone? There are two ways in which people interpret this; either that you fear someone because you respect them, and you do not want to disappoint them or else if you do, they may punish you. Well, fear of the lord is totally different. When you fear the lord, you give him deep respect, reverence and high esteem to his authority and power. We fear the lord not because he is not going to reward or punish us if we do not, but because he deserves it as the mighty creator of us and everything around us that we enjoy on Earth. Although he is pleased with those who fear him, and reward them for doing so, he is not going to punish or kill those who don't fear him. He deserves the fear as our father just as we fear our Earthly fathers. You see when your Earthly father is annoyed with you, he is not going to kill or punish you because you have disrespected him. Yes, indeed your Earthly father may be displeased with you because you have disrespected him, but he is not going to hit you on the head with a sledgehammer. This is exactly what the fear of the lord means. He deserves his reverent fear by us, and he wishes us well when we fear him. So, it is good fear not bad fear. Sometimes he may discipline us, but it is not for bad, but our own good. In fact, it is for our good that we must fear him.

The same God who asked us to fear not, is the one who is asking us to fear him. The Bible is very clear God has not given us the Spirit of fear but of love, power and of sound mind. God does not want us to fear dangerous things of the world such as Earthquakes, storms, tsunamis, accidents, sicknesses, wars, fire and flood, bacteria and viruses, people, diseases, demons and Satan himself. The fear of these things is unnecessary fear, and it can paralyse us not to function properly even before they happen to us. These are the things God want us not to fear. The fear of these things can destroy us. This is not the fear God demands from us, but rather a fear of respect for him as our father. Whether we are right or wrong he still loves us, as our father, just as our Earthly fathers do. If we are fearful not to disappoint those people, we respect the most, then we must also do the same for our father and our creator, the living God.

There are benefits that come with fear of the lord; things such as long life, power, peace, love, joy, and many other blessings. Even as we are blessed by him with these heavenly blessings, we must continue to fear him by checking and examining ourselves throughout our stay here on Earth. We must continue to check on our thoughts, actions, and words in order not to go astray from his "will," for us. This is the true beginning of wisdom. True wisdom is about having knowledge and understanding of God's ways. Every single decision we make every day must correspond with the "will" of God for our lives. This is the true fear of God. If we respect people, we are careful not to harm their feelings for us and for themselves.

GOD'S WILL

What is God's will? It is what he wants us to do for him, not for ourselves. Sometimes as Christians we focus too much on what God can do for us and not what we can do for God. Yes, indeed God as our creator has a plan for us, and it is safer for us to stay within his will for us. This may be confusing or complicating but let me put it this way; God's plan for us is what he thinks is good for us, not what we think is good for ourselves. For example, God loves us and that is why he had to send his son to die for us. But this has a string attached to it, which is that we must believe in his son to have life and to thereafter, obtain our salvation. If we want to have salvation, then we must believe in his son Jesus Christ, to be saved. If we don't, then we may be condemned. This is the best example I can give within the "will" of God in which we can be saved. We can never be saved outside this "will" of his for us.

Furthermore, God wants us above all else to first seek his Kingdom and its righteousness, for everything else to be added to us (Mathew 6:33). It is his will that every one of his children seek him first before he can bless them with his heavenly blessings. Why does God want us to first seek his Kingdom before everything else? It is inherent within our human nature that we accept blessings or gifts from the people we know very well. Very rarely do we accept gifts from strangers. The same thing applies to God; he does not want to give to the people who don't know him. God is in the business of revealing himself to his children for the following reasons; firstly he is the creator of the universe and he wants his children to know him as such; secondly he want us to communicate with him daily; thirdly, he want us to respect his laws and judgements and live by them; fourthly he wants to assign to us our heavenly assignments; fifth he want us to be a blessing to others when we know him, and sixth he wants to release to us our heavenly blessings from him. Blessings of God without his full knowledge on our part can destroy us. For example, if God had to bless you today with millions of dollars what would you do with it? I may not know exactly what you would use it on, but it is most likely going to be on yourself- buying expensive mansions, foods and services, cars, clothes, boats, planes and so much more. All these things have nothing to do with God. Yes, these things are of God, but they are not God's agenda for us. They are all bonuses when we know God's agenda for us. Let me say this hypothetically. After you have had knowledge of God, and he blesses you with millions of dollars, your thinking and spending will be totally different. Yes, indeed you may spend a big chuck on yourself, but you will also give to the poor, widows, orphans and the disabled in the community. You will also spend some of the money on building churches, schools, and communication television to reach out to people with God's gospel of salvation. You see the same money but have different thinking about how to spend it.

Perhaps the person we can refer to about God's will and the fear of God in the bible was St Paul, who was caught up doing his human will and not God's will when he was persecuting

Christians. He took it upon himself to kill Christians, thinking that he was doing it for God, yet he was doing it for himself and his fellow Pharisees. He was killing Christians thinking that he was protecting Jewish religion, which was God's religion, when it was not. He continued behaving this way until God revealed himself and his agenda to him in a dramatic way, while Saul was on his way to Damascus to kill Christians. What he was doing before God revealed himself to, Paul, was not God's agenda and God's plan for him. In a dramatic way God had to reveal his call to him, which was to preach the gospel to the Gentiles. This is exactly what we do today. We may be doing what we think may be good for us, yet it is our own will. Unless God reveals his agenda for us, we may be tempted to do our own will thinking it is God's will for us. With the fear of God in our lives he can reveal his plan for us, not in a dramatic way, as it was done to St Paul, but peacefully.

Acts 9:3 As he journeyed he came near Damascus, and suddenly a light shone around him from heaven. 4 Then he fell to the ground, and heard a voice saying to him, "Saul, Saul, why are you persecuting Me?" 5 And he said, "Who are You, Lord?" Then the Lord said, "I am Jesus, whom you are persecuting. 15 But the Lord said to him, "Go, for he is a chosen vessel of Mine to bear My name before Gentiles, kings, and the children of Israel. NKJV.

When we fear God, he does not reveal his will to us in a dramatic way like he did with St Paul. St Paul had no fear of God in him when he was persecuting Christians. He thought he was doing it for God, and he had no reason to fear God. St Paul had no personal relationship with God, yet he assumed he was working for God. There is no way you can work for someone you do not know and have no relationship with. For example, our lord Jesus Christ came into the world in human flesh to reveal the will of God to us. His primary objective was to restore the kingdom of God, lost through Adam, back to us. Through Christ, God, had to reconcile himself back to humanity through the death of his son on the cross for our sins in the flesh. Even as God has offered this gracious gift of salvation through his son, people continue to reject it and they continue to die through their sins today. He gave us his son to die in our place for our sins, in order to set us free from the law of sin and death into the law of righteousness through Christ. It is the will of God that everyone be saved, but they must be saved through their belief in his son Jesus Christ. There is no way you can reject Christ and expect God's salvation.

God wants us to live and grow within his will for us in order that we can become his children. He wants us to fear him, walks in his ways, love him, worship him and to serve him with our souls, hearts, and strength. Whenever our actions and words are not within his will for us then we must quickly realign them to his will if we are to see or achieve meaningful progress in our service for him. Every time there is confusion and dilemma in your mind for the will of God then you must seek him in prayer and fasting and reading the bible. God will clearly always communicate his will to us. This can be through the bible, voice, prophecy, visions and dreams and other signs and wonders. On many occasions God has been able to reveal his will for us through dreams, yet we do not always pay close attention to them. The living God is our true father, and he will always reveal his will for us.

LAWS

When we fear the lord, we obey his commandments and live by them. We must observe the commandments if we love him with our minds, souls, and spirits and love our fellow human beings as ourselves. If we fear him then we are careful not to disappoint him by breaking his laws. Just as there are consequences for breaking naturals laws in nations, societies and communities, there are also consequences for breaking God laws. For example, in a nation when you break the law of life by killing someone, you will be arrested, taken to court, and judged and imprisoned for life. At the same time God is not going to be happy with our action, and there will be a penalty with him for murder. God is not happy with us today for abortions which is the killing of unborn babies. We have broken God's law of life by killing unborn children with no proper medical reasons. He is also not happy because we have broken his law of marriage. We know according to him, that marriage is between one man and one woman. What do we have today? A marriage between one woman and one woman and one man and one man. This is an abomination to the lord. Sexual immorality is one of the things God hates the most. In fact, it is one of the reasons among others why he destroyed Sodom and Gomorrah. There is no longer reverent fear of God today in our world with respect to his laws. In fact, the ten commandments were given to us for our own good. God's laws are there to show us our sins in order that we may avoid them. If we observe and obey them, we can live by them. For your easy remembrance, these laws are summarised into two: love the lord your God with all your soul, heart and energy and love your neighbour as yourself.

JUDGEMENT

Unfortunately, there is an anticipated judgement of God over those who reject the gospel of salvation and those who sin wilfully against God. Those who treat God's message of salvation with contempt, those who are not sure there is a God (agnostics), and those who think there is no God (atheists), have subjected themselves to the waiting judgement of God, if they do not change their minds before they die. What happens when people reject God? They live a sinful lifestyle that brings unexpected judgement of God on them. No matter who we are, there is a propensity to commit sin because of our sinful nature as human beings. If we are not cautious or when we do not show remorse and repent for our sins, we can be judged. God does not look away from the sins people commit, and they will be judged because of their unrepented sins.

It is important to know that Satan was judged and sentenced to life imprisonment because of his sin against God. He wanted to be like God and so he waged a rebellious war in heaven against God. He lost together with his angels, and they were cast to the Earth. If God punished his angels who had sinned, then what do you think of our own sin? Sin is punishable by death according to God. Those who do not fear God will be punished for their sins, which will be permanent isolation from him.

1 Corinthians 6:9 Do you not know that the unrighteous will not inherit the kingdom of God? Do not be deceived. Neither fornicators, nor idolaters, nor adulterers, nor homosexuals, nor sodomites, 10 nor thieves, nor covetous, nor drunkards, nor revilers, nor extortioners will inherit the kingdom of God. NKJV.

All these sins are punishable by death. Christians are not immune from these sins too, if they live unrepentant lifestyles or if they commit them wilfully. God sent his son to die for our sins to correct our sins in the flesh. If you reject what Christ has done for your sins, then unfortunately no one else will die for your sins but you. Think about that. If you continue to commit sin wilfully as Christians, then there is nothing else left for you but the judgement of God. Today people and nations have brought upon themselves judgment of God due to sinful lifestyle and wilful commitment of sins. There is nothing God hates more than the worshipping of idols, bloodshed, sexual immorality, injustice, greed, corruption, deception and lying. You must make sure that there is no any of these sins in you if you are a Christian. These sins, if unrepented, can also attract demons to possess us, even if we are born-again Christians. It is only the presence of the Holy Spirit within us that can scare away the demons. The Holy Spirit cannot be in a person who loves sins and who lives a sinful lifestyle.

STATUTES

Statutes are God's written laws. There are God's written laws in the Bible and in our own hearts. The laws governing our consciences are written in our hearts. They are written to govern our internal moral conduct, where human laws have no ability to govern the conduct of people. That is why God knows our thoughts before they become our speech and actions. The ability to judge between what is right or wrong, lies within every single human being, who is mature. That is why from the age of thirteen years and above we are held responsible for our own actions. Before we can do right or wrong, we are sure exactly of what we are doing, even though we can later deny it, if it gets us into trouble. No human being can deny this assertion. For example, our lord Jesus Christ warned us not to commit adultery by looking at a woman lustfully (Mathew 5:28). What does this mean? Our thoughts get us to commit adultery before our action. Before we attempt to go and sleep with her, we would have committed adultery already by looking at her lustfully and by wishing to sleep with her in our thoughts. Furthermore, when Christ was on Earth, he was able to detect the religious leaders' and disciples' thoughts before they spoke to him. He knew exactly what they were thinking in their minds before they spoke their words. People who commit sin know exactly what they are doing before they do it. They know that certain words or actions will lead them into committing sin, yet they go ahead and commit sin by ignoring the still voice of the Holy Spirit, within them. It is after they have committed sin that they get convicted by the Holy Spirit and they come to the realisation that they have committed sin. We do not have to be told by somebody else that we are committing sin, as we are fully aware of it before we commit it.

The reverent fear of God deep within us enables us to live a sinless lifestyle because we are aware that God knows our thoughts inside us. People who fear God will honour him with their service and worship. It is very hard for those who fear God to commit sin and to also allow the sinful nature to dominate their lives. More importantly those who allow the Holy Spirit to live within them cannot commit sin, because he will tip them off beforehand. For example, there will be a warning by the Holy Spirit through the word of knowledge, vision and mission or revelation, about the sin we are about to commit. Those who are mature in the things of God, know what I am talking about. We must give glory to God through our service and worship. When we serve God with our resources, energy and time, he can be proud of us, and he will reward us openly.

OBEDIENCE

There is reward for those who are obedient to God. For example, our lord Jesus Christ was obedient to God to the point of death, and he was rewarded for it. Although he was God, he humbled himself and accepted to die on our behalf to reconcile us back to God. Through his obedience he was able to endure shame, pain, ridicule, insults, isolation, betrayal, denial, and death on our own behalf. Just for us to have life. Because of this he was given the name above every name in heaven and on Earth and all creation was handed over to him. The same thing happens to those who are obedient to God; they are rewarded with wealth, long life, honour, wisdom, understanding and knowledge. Those Christians who live in reverent awe of God will be protected by God no matter what happens to them.

Job was a good example of those individuals. He was encouraged by his wife to curse God and die, and he was also accused by his friends of having committed sin, which was the reason he suffered. But he did not sin either by his words or his actions, and God backed him up. Because of his fear of God, he came out victorious over his enemies without sinning and he was rewarded for it. Integrity was one of the strong weapons Job used against his enemies. We must use our strong Christian values to defeat our enemies including Satan and his demons.

Christian values such as compassion, love, endurance, perseverance, kindness, peace, and calmness are important for our battle in this world against our enemies.

WILLINGNESS

Our willingness to serve God must come voluntarily from us due to our love and fear of him. Are we willing to go on God's mission without rejecting or resisting the call by God to do so, like Jonah did? Are we able to do things for God without expecting rewards in return like Dorcus/Tabatha? We know Dorcus was raised from death by God through Peter because of her prior services to the poor. The people she had sewn clothes for cried out to the lord, and she was raised from death as a reward for her services to the people of God – the poor.

Those who preach the gospel of our lord Jesus Christ to the world have a reward from the lord. Within every generation on Earth, his servants are called out for the work of God, yet many reject their call in the preference for their own works and their other engagements of this life. Even those who have accepted to do the work of God, want to know their rewards before they even go to the field for harvest. I was one of those who rejected this great call to preach the word for a very long time, yet God was patient with me. I am happy that I have accepted this call today to be a preacher of good news to the world.

There is nothing more pleasing than to bring the gospel of our lord Jesus Christ to those who are perishing. The good news of salvation through the preaching of the gospel saves lives from going to hell. It is the greatest honour for me to be part of the team that helps in the spreading of the gospel. I am grateful to God for bringing me in to his kingdom of life.

6

YOUR BODY; THE TEMPLE OF THE HOLY SPIRIT IN YOU

John 3:16 For God so loved the world that He gave His only begotten Son, that whoever believes in Him should not perish but have everlasting life.

What used to kill mankind in the flesh was the sin in the flesh. The sin in the flesh had given Satan the power to kill humans. When Jesus Christ came in the flesh, he had to defeat the sin in the flesh, on behalf of human beings, giving them the ability to resurrect and to go and live with God forever. As Christians me must continue to celebrate Christ for this victory on our own behalf. Your sins are now forgiven through the blood of Jesus Christ, and you can now live a life of repentance before God every day.

No one has a monopoly on God; all Christians can have God within themselves if they can choose to activate the Holy Spirit within themselves. There is a Spirit of God available to all who are interested in the salvation of their souls. You can choose to have your own experiential knowledge of God before you die. You do not need to die to later discover there is a God. It will be too late by then. Seek him wholeheartedly and he will reveal himself to you.

THE MEANING OF THE TEMPLE

Before we can proceed with our discussion, we must first understand the concept and meaning of the temple. If I may ask you, what is the meaning of temple to you and what is your understanding of it? Well, I would love to hear your answers but let me give you a brief definition and meaning of the temple; it is a building in which God is worshipped. Furthermore, if you like, it is a building that hosts the presence of God during peoples' worship.

Throughout the history of humanity God has made his existence and presence known to the peoples of Earth. To put it simply there is no tribe, community, society, and nation in which people have no knowledge and existence of God. With this knowledge of his existence, peoples of Earth must bow down in honouring his existence through worship. In many places today around the world people have designated places such as mountains, rivers, shrines, caves, temples, and churches for worshipping him. People have also used many symbols such as sun, moon, stars plants and animals as forms of worshipping him. God has put the desires and knowledge of himself in people's hearts in order that they might worship him. People, also out of curiosity and fear of dangers, were forced to seek answers from the supernatural world. In doing this, they bow down to worship God.

Let us go back to the concept and meaning of the temple. Temple is a building in which God is worshipped. But the next question is where did the temple originate from? And from which people? Why is it the only word common in the Bible representing the building for worshipping God? The temple can be traced to the Israelites, who still worship God today in the temple. This does mean that there are no other peoples of Earth who worship God in the temple. The idea that God can be worshipped in a temple came from them. The reason why "temple" is the common word in the Bible today is the fact that it was the Israelites who had the ability to write their languages including the ability to write the Bible and their ways of worship. For example, we learn from the Bible that the idea of worshipping God in a temple (physical building) came from King David, who did not build the temple himself because God did not allow him to do so, but his vision and dream was later fulfilled by his son Solomon, who built the temple for the Lord almighty. Right from the patriarch Abraham to King David, Israelites used to worship God in places such as Bethel through a mobile tabernacle (temple), which hosted the presence of God.

In a nutshell, the temple is the Israelites' building of worship, which is also equivalent to today's Christian churches of worship. In temple or church, there is a manifestation of the presence of God. When people go to church or temple, they go to worship and serve God. While in the temple or church, people can worship and serve God in forms of prayers, singing of songs, praises, dancing, dedication, baptism, repentance, testimonies, contributions and more importantly to hear the word of God. All these acts of worship and faith in the existence of God, are a good example as to why people need to have the temple or church for worshipping God.

THE PURPOSE OF THE TEMPLE

If you are following me very keenly you will know I have given two definitions of the temple or church, one being the building and the other being a building that hosts the presence of God. Now let me take you through my favourite definition of the temple or the church, which is the second definition, that defines the temple or church as being the building that hosts the presence of God. The simple reason why I like the second definition is the fact that temple or church without the presence of God is nothing. There must be the presence of God in a temple or church for it to have meaning. You can go to a church or a temple to worship, but if the presence of God is not there, then you have no-worship at all. If we go to church we expect to hear from God, that is the only way we can have complete assurances that God exists and can listen to our prayers. The reason for going to church or a temple is more important than just entering the physical building without purpose. If you go to church or temple and never hear from God, then you have entered a physical building that has no purpose or benefits to you. When we go to church or temple, we expect to hear from God who can answer our prayers of provisions (food and water, clothes, shelter, house), protection (security, peace, joy, love healing and guidance) and worship (hearing the words of hope, faith, mercy, compassion and praises and songs and dancing that make us happy). If you go to a physical building and not find the mentioned benefits, then there is no presence of God in that church, and you would not have heard from God. You can continue to go into that church for several years and you will not have your own experiential knowledge with God, because

God is not a physical building, but a spirit who can make his presence known in a physical building. You cannot worship a God that does not speak to you; it will be a waste of time. A church that does not host the presence of God, is a not church and you must quit such a church, in search for the right one that hosts the presence of God. Furthermore, the physical building that hosts the presence of God is not the right church but is a good starting point in your quest for the right church. This question may have popped up into your mind already: What is the right church then, if the physical building that hosts the presence of God is not the right Church?

YOUR BODY IS THE RIGHT TEMPLE FOR GOD

While God was preparing our bodies of sin for his Holy Spirit to dwell within us, he had to introduce the concept of a physical building that would host his presence in a form of the temple or church. Before the Holy Spirit was assigned to individuals, there was a need for a physical location that would host the presence of God for those who would worship him. Now through the death of our Lord Jesus Christ, our sins have been cleansed and the Holy Spirit can dwell within our bodies, as the true temple of God. Those Christians who live a sinless lifestyle, together with those who repent and show remorse for their sins, are considered by God as holy ground in which the Spirit of God can dwell. The Spirit of God becomes your friend if you allow him to dwell in you and he can teach the things of heaven to you. You become a contact point between heaven and Earth. What a blessing to become the contact point for God and his people.

Let me be clear it is still important to go to church and pray to God in unison as Christians. Church or temple are still important places for Christians to meet to share the word of God together. But here is the difference between you being the temple of God and the physical building being the temple of God; now God lives in you and no longer in a physical building in a certain location where you can meet him to hear from him. Furthermore, when the Holy Spirit is in you, you are now hosting the presence of God daily instead of one weekly Sunday or Saturday worship. You now have your one-on-one encounters with God instead of just the Sunday sermon by your Pastor. There is a difference between hearing the voice of God from other people and hearing it directly from within you. The reasons many people doubt the existence of God is because they have had no personal encounters with him. The only way you can never doubt the existence of God is to have your own individual encounters and experiential knowledge of him. When you have encounters with God individually in forms of a voice, dream, vision, prophesy, revelation, wonders, and signs, you will never doubt his existence ever again. It was a promise of God that his spirit will have one-on-one encounters with us when he was to be sent to the Earth. This promise became a reality on the day of Pentecost, when the Holy Spirit came and descended on those individuals present in Jerusalem.

Acts-17-19 'And it shall come to pass in the last days, says God, That I will pour out of My Spirit on all flesh; Your sons and your daughters shall prophesy, Your young men shall see visions, Your old men shall dream dreams. And on My menservants and on My maidservants I will pour out My Spirit in those days; And they shall prophesy. I will show wonders in heaven above And signs in the Earth beneath: Blood and fire and vapor of smoke. NKJV

It is critical to note some few important things in these verses that apply to all of us. Firstly, God did not promise to pour out his spirit on a physical temple or church, but on his people, which is you and me. Secondly, the prophecies, visions, dreams and many other wonderful signs, will become common language of the day for those who would allow the spirit of God to dwell within them. Other wonderful signs of the presence of God within individuals such as healing of the sick, raising the dead, speaking in tongues, word of knowledge about individuals' situations and conditions and other important miracles will become available to those who would carry the presence of God wherever they are. How beautiful is it that the same Holy Spirit of God who enabled our Lord Jesus Christ to perform all the miracles, is available to us today? How beautiful is it to reach out to your brothers and sisters who have had no opportunity to hear the word of God, to reach out to them with the help of Holy Spirit? How beautiful is it for you to be a station through which God can reveal the mysteries of the kingdom of heaven in order to reach out to the rest of humanity? How beautiful is it for God to choose you among the millions of people on Earth to reach out to the rest of humanity? Now there is an opportunity for you to take up your cross and follow our Lord Jesus Christ. Wise, is the man who wins souls. How wonderful will it be to go to heaven with some of your family members, relatives, friends, colleagues, and other members of the public who will heed your message of salvation?

YOUR BODY AS AN OPERATIONS TEMPLE FOR THE GODHEAD

Once you have repented of your sins and have accepted our Lord Jesus Christ as your personal saviour through the baptism of water, the next move is to be baptised with the Holy Spirit through the laying on of hands by men and women filled with the Holy Spirit. After these important steps have been completed, your body now becomes a temple of the Holy Spirit. Your body is now the church of God not the physical building. You begin to hear from God now on daily basis not weekly or monthly basis of gathering in the church–a physical building.

On many occasions Christians do not pay attention to what is happening within themselves, even when they have been baptised with the Holy Spirit. That is why they miss out on what God is trying to tell them. God is a spirit, and we cannot see him physically. This is not to say that he cannot manifest in the physical realm. Jesus Christ himself was a spirit but he had to manifest in physical form, because there was a need to do so. Furthermore, the Holy Spirit manifests himself sometimes in form of a fire, a dove, a wind, and water. His manifestation in these forms does not mean that he is these forms. They can choose to manifest in these forms if there is a need, but not always. But that is not what I am saying. If you are going to focus on the physicality, then you will miss out on the spirituality. What is happening inside you is a lot bigger than what is happening outside you.

If you want to hear from the Godhead, then you must pay attention to your inner-most being – particularly your spirit. We will talk about this in detail in the next chapter on the human spirit. When you want to know the presence of God in you, then you must pay attention to your spirit – what is happening inside you. Focus on your thoughts, dreams, visions, and revelations, and what you will gain out of these encounters will blow your mind. Reduce the physical activities of Earth and focus on the spiritual activities of heaven and you will see heaven manifesting in you. Our Lord Jesus Christ spoke about this very clearly, that the world will neither see the Holy Spirit nor him, because they cannot. The people in the world cannot see the Godhead because they focus on the physicality over the spirituality. Furthermore, the world does not keep the commandments of our Jesus Christ and so he has no reason to manifest to the world and the people in the world. But he will manifest himself to those who believe in him and keep his commandments; these are the born-again Christians. The fountains of living waters will flow out of the bellies of those who believe-and keep the commandments of our lord Jesus Christ. The Spirit of God is life to those who have him. Out of their Spirits, they will experience amongst other things, peace, grace, love, joy, wisdom, knowledge, understanding, power, discernment, and revelations that the world does not have, nor does it give to its children.

We as human beings take pride in what we have done or what we can do, because of our self-belief and capabilities. This may be sometimes due to our physical looks or our internal capabilities such as knowledge, wisdom, understanding and power that is beyond and above others. But this is all fleshly philosophical thinking that has no basis at all. We take pride in our capabilities that can be short-lived if you do not acknowledge God, who has placed within us all these gifts. It is God who has given us all forms of gifts for our own good and the good of others, but we must acknowledge him as the source of all gifts to humanity and to us. For example, those that have not been given knowledge have no knowledge. Those that have not been given wisdom and understanding have no wisdom and understanding. This is a simple fact. Should we take pride in what is not ours? Definitely not. The difference between the children of God and the children of the world is that the children of God acknowledge this fact, and they are humbled.

God only teaches the humble. The reason why many Christians do not experience the kingdom of God within themselves even when they have been baptised with the Holy Spirit, is the fact they are prideful. For example, many teachers of the gospel today think that they are better teachers because of their theological knowledge and training, and as such, ignore the teaching of the Holy Spirit. This is completely wrong thinking and people with this mentality will never give the Holy Spirit an opportunity to teach them. The Holy Spirit of God remains the supreme teacher of the Bible and all things about the kingdom of God. The only way we can receive from God is when we are humble and commit to the teaching of the Holy Spirit. In the natural context, a student cannot teach his teacher no matter how intelligent that student may be. We cannot teach things of God without the help of God. It doesn't work. In fact, St Paul addressed this wrong thinking in his letter to the Ephesians, that it is only God within us who can do exceedingly above what we ask or think. Unless we acknowledge that it is God who has given power to do everything we do well, then we are denying ourselves more opportunities of his teachings. Unless we acknowledge that it is God who has given us an opportunity to do well and seek after his teachings, then we will not do well. In both ends, we need God's teachings for us to continue to do well and more importantly to continue to receive more from him. There will always be more for those who are hungry and thirsty for his knowledge and his teachings. The depth, height, width and length of his knowledge surpasses all human understanding, no matter who we think we are. The knowledge of God is granted to those who are humble and who are committed to be taught by the Holy Spirit.

Ephesians 3:20-21 Now to Him who is able to do exceedingly abundantly above all that we ask or think, according to the power that works in us, to Him be glory in the church by Christ Jesus to all generations, forever and ever. NKJV.

Let me touch on a few things St Paul is saying here in these verses to the Ephesians. Firstly, he is saying that the only way they can experience the glory of God within their churches (which are their bodies), is to allow his power to work within them. Secondly, when they allow the Spirit of God to work within them, he will work beyond their expectations, knowledge, wisdom and their understanding. Just as St Paul enjoyed the abundance of God's grace, mercy, faith, power and strength, he found it to be endless and inexhaustible, because he was committed to the teachings of the Holy Spirit. There is an abundance of riches in God's kingdom that we must commit to have as we work for him. St Paul was filled with the fullness of God, and we should be filled with the same fullness of God, as born-again Christians. There is always more in God than in us and we must strive to get that fullness. Never underestimate yourself because you serve a big God. Always think big because you serve a big God, and the big God will surprise you bigly.

SELF-IMAGE

Born-again Christians no longer see themselves as themselves. Those who have allowed the Holy Spirit to live within them no longer have complete independent control of their bodies as it is the temple of the Holy Spirit. Those who have accepted the lordship of Jesus Christ over their bodies have surrendered their bodies to the control of the Holy Spirit. What they think, what they do, what they speak and the character they exhibit to the world is no longer their former selves but that of Christ who lives in them.

2 Corinthians 5:17 Therefore, if anyone is in Christ, he is a new creation; old things have passed away; behold, all things have become new. NKJV.

Being a new creation in Christ, means having a new way of thinking and new way of doing things according to the kingdom of heaven principles, values, norms, laws and regulations. For example, the kingdom of heaven principles are righteousness, mercy, faithfulness, justice, truth, compassion, honesty, integrity, purity and humbleness. Born-again Christians must apply these principles in their daily living. In addition, the Christian-values such as love, peace, kindness, goodness, gentleness and self-control also become part of the new person in Christ. All born-again Christians are ambassadors of the kingdom of heaven on Earth. We must stand up and protect these Christian principles and values on Earth. We must be proud of who we are as kingdom of God citizens on Earth. We must represent the best of our nation (heaven) on Earth. Think about it; if you don't stand up for what you believe and what you love, then who else will? If we don't stand up and speak up for our lord Jesus Christ now, how will he stand up for us in heaven in this life and the next life to come? If we are ashamed of Christ, how will Christ not be ashamed of us in the life to come?

Following my conversations with many Christians in conferences, seminars, meetings, pulpits and many other Christians forums, believers have had mixed reactions in defense of Christian principles and values against encroaching secularism. In the pushed for an inclusive society, secularists have accused religious institutions and Christians of being exclusive and discriminatory based on their values and norms. For example, secularists have argued against Christian values and principles on marriage, abortion, gender, race, colour among other things. The secularists have used these cards wrongly to advance their sinister evil agenda on human society. The opposite is true. Christians values and principles have advanced the sense of togetherness of human society over years. Hence, the principle of the good Samaritan has led to the pooling of resources to look after the poor in society. There are many Christian organisations today looking after the poor in the society in giving aid, scholarships, protection and provisions of refuge to the refugees. Furthermore, Christian values of love, peace, kindness, compassion, mercy and justice have helped hold human society together particularly in the diverse nations.

We have the responsibility as Christians to advance and proclaim the kingdom of heaven's message to the whole world. In fact, the idea of globalisation is Christian ideology as it was our lord Jesus Christ who first came up with this ideology. We are the light of the world, and we must continue to be so until our lord Jesus Christ's return. We must preach the gospel to win souls to Christ out of the sinking world.

Matthew 28: 18-20 Then Jesus came to them and said, "All authority in heaven and on Earth has been given to me. [19] Therefore go and make disciples of all nations, baptizing them in the name of the Father and of the Son and of the Holy Spirit, [20] and teaching them to obey everything I have commanded you. And surely I am with you always, to the very end of the age.» NIV.

With words, actions and our character we must be conscious of the fact that the Holy Spirit lives within us. Now that we have been made aware that the Spirit of God lives within us, we must be careful of what we think, speak, do and what we show to others through our self-conduct. By this I mean that the words we speak, what we think, the actions we take and the character we show to others must matched with the character of the Holy Spirit. If we have allowed the Holy Spirit to live inside us, then our role is reduced to that of a spoke person. We speak and act on behalf of heaven and particularly on behalf of the Holy Spirit. What we speak and do is not our own but what we are told by the Holy Spirit. For example, in the world, the presidential spokesperson speaks on behalf of the president of a nation and the business spokesperson speaks on behalf of the business company. That does not mean that these people cannot speak for themselves sometimes, but it is only in a private forum or function where they are not officially on duty. But they come out and distinguish themselves when they speak at a private function, and they are not speaking on behalf of the president or the business. But their conduct even in the private function must reflect the office they hold.

Matthew 10:18-20-You will be brought before governors and kings for My sake, as a testimony to them and to the Gentiles. But when they deliver you up, do not worry about how or what you should speak. For it will be given to you in that hour what you should speak; for it is not you who speak, but the Spirit of your Father who speaks in you. **NKJV.**

Sometimes the presidential and business spokespersons get into trouble because of the offices they hold and the presidents and the businesses they represent to the public. They can be loved or hated by the public because of their actions, conducts and words. When they get into problems, they are not worried about what to say, as they go back to the president or business and consult with senior leadership on how to address the problem.

The same thing applies to us, who speak on behalf of heaven. We can be persecuted for the message of salvation we carry with us through the Earth. We can be hated because of the word. In fact, Jesus Christ warned us that we are liable and subject to persecution because of the words and his name's sake. When this happens, we must not be worried about what we should say to these Earthly authorities who can persecute us for the word of God, as the Holy Spirit, speaks through us. In fact, through our words inspired by the Holy Spirit, we can be a testimony to the authorities that the kingdom of heaven is within us by what we say and do. In fact, at that moment, persecution becomes an opportunity to bring the message of salvation to people. We have seen this in the bible with St Paul and the Roman authorities. Every time he was persecuted or put in prison; it was an opportunity for him to preach the word of God to them. We saw it when he was jailed with Silas; they converted the prison security guard into a follower of our Jesus Christ, through their actions and conduct. Paul goes further and even puts it boldly, "I am in chains, but the word of God is not in chains." St Paul had to use his persecution and imprisonment as an opportunity to bring as many people as possible from the prison into the kingdom of God. St Paul is telling us today that it doesn't matter where we are on Earth, we can use persecution to bring people to the kingdom of God, by preaching the good news of salvation to our persecutors.

Contrastingly, even though the Holy Spirit is within us, he is an independent minded spiritual being, meaning that he works autonomously according to the policies of heaven. If we cannot respect the Holy Spirit and live according to the standards of heaven he requires from us, then he can either leave us or go silent within us. As our bodies become the temple of the Holy Spirit, we must continue to worship, and always revere and honour him. Therefore, what we let into our bodies is so critical for the Holy Spirit. The words we speak, the actions we take and the way we behave is also observed by the Holy Spirit. He will tell us when we are right and wrong, when we pay attention to his instructions. Remember this always, that the Holy Spirit is a person with emotions, and he can be grieved or quenched by our unpleasing conduct, every time we commit an unlawful action. That is why St Paul had to warn the Ephesians to get rid of their old selfish nature such as anger, bitterness, quarrelling, gossip, lying, fornication, idol worship, sexual immorality, slander, violence, injustice, greed, corruption, tribalism, racism and all forms of malice. All these human sins not only grieve the Holy Spirit, but they also make him quit us. These are from the sinful nature of our old selves before we were baptised with the Holy Spirit, and we must get rid of them all if we are to be heaven conscious and destined. We must treat our bodies as sacred shrines of which the Holy Spirit can be please, as it would be in the church you go to. While in the church (physical building), worshipping God, you always exhibit good character in the presence of others, and more importantly in respect to God whom you worship.

It is also important to note that we must not only look after our bodies because they are the temple of the Holy Spirit, but also for our own good. A healthy body means a healthy you. For this reason, we must look after our bodies in terms of what we eat and drink, as well as exercise and good sleep habits. For example, Jews were well known for looking after their bodies. Jews will not eat unless they have washed their hands, whenever they go to the market. It was their tradition passed down from generation to generation. They kept it because it was good for them. In terms of today's science, it is a healthy recommended habit by world standards. But what was their problem? Why was our Jesus Christ, so critical of them? Because they looked after their external bodies more than their internal bodies. They refused to allow the kingdom of God to enter them and change them on the inside, then the outside. Our take-away from their actions is that we must look at both our external and internal bodies. We must look at what is happening inside us and outside us, if we are to be good temples of the Holy Spirit.

If God was not mindful of what to put into our bodies, he would have not warned us about plants and animals to eat and not to eat. In terms of sexual immorality, St Paul warned the Corinthians to be mindful of what went into their bodies, which is also a warning to us today. Particularly, sexual immorality is one of the sins that defiles our bodies. In fact, it has the potential to kill us if we are not careful. For instance, many sexual transmitted diseases such as HIV-aids, syphilis, gonorrhoea, hepatitis, herpes and chlamydia, have the potential to destroy our bodies, or for that matter kill us.

We are not only talking about sexual immorality, but also other ill-conceived human behaviours influenced by the devil in order to destroy our bodies. These include excessive drug and alcohol abuse, pornography, masturbation, sodomy, cutting and piercing, modelling, and other forms of starvation of our bodies. Take for example, modelling; women and particularly young girls have starved themselves of food and drinks for the sake of beauty. They have been told by celebrities to believe that beauty lies in being skinny. Not only do young girls abstain from certain food and drinks that are important for their bodily nutrients, but also sometimes take weight loss drugs that do damage to important organs within their bodies, endangering their future careers, and perhaps even their life. Once the magnitude of this damage has been done to a human body it can never be reversed. This is not to say that you must quit modelling as a young girl, but you must do it without endangering your health. You cannot starve your body of food, which also denies your body of important nutrients for its looks and healthy. You can never re-create your body outside as it was already given to you by God, not only beautiful, but also wonderfully made.

In short, we must honour God with our bodies, because he created them to host his Spirit – the Holy Spirit. Even though we are in our bodies, they are not our own. They are sacred shrines for the Holy Spirit. If God was not serious about our bodies, he wouldn't have redeemed them through the blood of his son Jesus Christ. Therefore, we must be careful of what we put into our bodies and what we bring out of them. Our bodies must be temples that reflect the character of God, in terms of kindness, compassion, mercy, justice, peace, love, joy, righteousness, rather than hatred, jealousy, bitterness, anger, envy, gossip, idol worship, bloodshed, and all forms of sexual immorality. Our bodies cannot be redeemed a second time by God once we choose to misuse them. Having read this chapter today on the human body, its function and purpose, the choice is yours; whose temple do you want to be – God's, or the devil's? I will leave it to you. But I must say this; God loves you, including your body.

7

YOUR SOUL; THE CONTROL CENTER OF THE HOLY SPIRIT IN YOU

What is the human soul? It is an immortal part of the human being. Soul is a combination of human spirit and body. It is what gives life to a human being. In other words, it is the life of a human being. When a human soul separates from the human body, a person is pronounced dead. The human soul is composed of human "will, mind/thoughts and emotions." In my other book called "Human being as a tripartite: body, soul and spirit", I have referred to the human soul as the deadliest weapon that God has ever given mankind. Why is this? Because it can choose to reject the very God who has given it to us. When this happens then we are dead. We will be like a soldier, who shot himself to death with his own gun, given to him by the government. Let me explain this analogy. A soldier is well trained and equipped by the government or the state on how to handle the gun, for his safety and his security, the security of others around him, the protection of the nation state from her enemies and the protection of the civil populace of that state. These are the purposes of which a soldier is given a gun, by the state or nation. The state thereafter is not responsible for any misuse or poor handling of the gun by the solider, including if he kills himself with it. The same thing applies to us as human beings. God has given us a human soul as a good weapon for our own good. You will probably appreciate the fact that the choices we make, and the emotions that drive them, are not all bad. These choices we make within our own souls may sometimes be independent of God. That is why God holds us accountable for such decisions and choices. It is a sincere wish of our creator that we do not misuse our souls. We have a responsibility to think, act and speak right within our souls. I don't think it would be in our best interests, if God had to dictate to us what we choose, think, speak or do, within our souls. What causes rebellion in the world today is when governments, businesses or our fellow human beings suppress or deny our choices and decisions.

A redeemed person no longer has his or her independent soul outside God. In fact, what caused the fall of Adam was the independence of his soul. Adam within his soul decided to reject God, and he sided with the devil because of his soul independence. The decision he took within his soul brought death upon him and the rest of his offspring. God corrected this through the death of our lord Jesus Christ on the cross for the sins of rebellious souls against him. God demands a new redeemed mankind to be obedient to him and to also serve him willingly. The new redeemed person no longer has independent thoughts, actions, words, and character that is contrary to God's agenda within their soul. In fact, God demands our souls to be loyal and to diligently serve him. Souls that come to Christ, now must repent of their sins, and be baptised with water for the remission of their sins, and to thereafter follow Christ wholeheartedly living a sinless life. Everyone who comes to Christ now must take his own cross and follow him.

Matthew 10:38-39 And he who does not take his cross and follow after Me is not worthy of Me. He who finds his life will lose it, and he who loses his life for My sake will find it. NKJV.

Following Christ is no longer optional; it is a must if you want to enter the kingdom of heaven. Christ is saying here, if you still choose not to follow me, then you are not worthy of me. In other words, he is saying if you still have a choice to make whether to follow me or not then you are not worthy of me. You have no value to add to why I came to the Earth. The invitation to pick up one's own cross and follow Jesus, places full responsibility on his followers who will preach the gospel of salvation, who will also expect persecutions that come with it. Christ took his own, when he was crucified for our sins to bring us to the kingdom of heaven. While he is now away, we have the responsibility to spread the message of salvation to win more souls to him. This is not an easy task, as it requires full commitment to the services of the kingdom of heaven. The cross represents the reproaches, persecutions, afflictions, abuses, hatred and all other ill-will from people who will oppose the message of salvation from us. In the worst-case scenario, Christ died carrying his own cross and we may also individually die carrying our own crosses. When you are called to carry your cross, you must cheerfully accept it, stick to its ordinances, and commit to suffer for the sake of it.

What about those who choose not to carry their own crosses?

Simply, these people have rejected the message of salvation. They have decided to find their lives and have saved them. And so, they are not worthy of Christ. They still have their right to exercise their "free will," not to follow Christ. These people have refused to forgo their current life of pleasures, enjoyment, and other sinful compliances with the world. Have refused to be persecuted, reproached, abused, and even shamefully put to death for the sake of Christ. Their primary focus is their own achievements and they have completely neglected the message of salvation through Christ. They have refused to be used by Christ and have chosen the pleasures of the current world instead of the coming world. They have refused to allow Christ into their temples to change their temples on the inside that they may be saved.

WILL

What is human will? It is the ability of a person to make their own choices without fear or influence by outside forces or people. It is simply the ability to do what you want. We must not take lightly the choices we make within our human will because what we choose becomes who we are and determines our future. We must take note of this! The choices, for example of the person you marry, and from what family, the religion you choose and its values and norms, the course you study as part of your career, the business to establish, the political party to join and its policies, the leadership you strive for, the job and the decisions you make as part of its operations, and the investment opportunities you take, are all determined by our human will. From the few mentioned choices, you can see how critical it is not to take our human will lightly because that is what our lives are dependent upon.

The concept of a free will has been illuminated in this verse for those who have chosen to take up their cross.

Galatians:2: 20 I have been crucified with Christ; it is no longer I who live, but Christ lives in me; and the life which I now live in the flesh I live by faith in the Son of God, who loved me and gave Himself for me. NKJV.

Let me start with the faith-based life we lived as Christians. Faith based life means we don't put our trust in our human will to make important decisions for our lives. The life we now live is based on our faith in Christ and the decisions we make are no longer made by us but Christ who lives within us in the person of the Holy Spirit. Before we make important decisions for our lives, we consult the Holy Spirit and what the Holy Spirit tells us about our important decisions, is our final decision. I know this may be very difficult for those who have had no encounter with the Holy Spirit, to leave the important decisions of your life with him. The person we don't know whether he will accept or reject the important decisions we are about to make. In addition, at times we want to make the decision very quickly and we don't want to involve the Holy Spirit. These are all valid reasons and arguments for not wanting to live a faith-based life but let me tell you this – it is worthwhile to live a faith-based life. Firstly, if we have accepted Christ then the life, we live is no longer lived according to us, but Christ. Secondly, Christ is the lord of yesterday, today, and tomorrow. Thirdly, he is the creator of us, and he knows everything about us and what is best for us. Fourthly, he has a better plan than we do for us and our lives.

Moreover, if Christ has loved us and has died for us, what then can he hold back from us? If he has given his life for us to have life, should he not be mindful about the life we lead here on Earth? He died for us for God to release for us the very things we crave for and chase after independently of him. Undoubtedly, he secured for us from God good health, wealth, power, wisdom, strength, honour, and glory. If we commit ourselves to Christ, all these things will follow us. They are bonuses for our commitment to the cause of Christ. We must preach the message of the kingdom, cast out demons, heal the sick, take up the serpents and God we will be pleased with us to release more of his blessings according to our immediate needs of the time. If we are within the will of God, then there is nothing he cannot do for us for his glory.

SELF-WILL

What is self-will? It is one's choice to make one's own decisions without taking advice from other people. The people who exercise the right of self-will speak this way; my life is mine, I don't share with anyone, I must live my life in the way I want, my life is no one's business, I know what I want for life, I oversee my future. People like this speak with absolute authority and power over their lives and what they can do and not do with it. They are lords over their lives and future. Although there is merit in running your own life the way you want, there is also merit in listening to advice and corrections of other people who may be important members of your family, community, society, and nation. Dangerously, people who live a self-willed life rule out God in the affairs of their lives. Why do I call it a dangerous move? Because there is no life and future without God, who created you, and the future you are talking about. God has even warned people who do this to immediately cease from doing it. For the simple reason it is he who oversees our lives, and he can choose to let our life continue or not if we don't acknowledge him as our creator.

God demands his children to prioritise his "will" not their "will" in everything they do. Christ, in the lord's prayer asked us to pray to God, "Your will be done on Earth as it is in heaven (Mathew 6:10)." You may ask, what is the "will" of God that is done in heaven and that needs to be done on Earth? Again, Christ has put it to us very clearly that we must love God with our own hearts, souls, minds, strength and we must love our neighbours as ourselves. Hence, the priority in the mind of the child of God is not about him or herself, but God and others. We love God when we hold dearly in our hearts his name, character, nature and his doctrines. He is holy and his children must be holy. He is worshipped and served in heaven, and we must do the same on Earth. We must here on Earth commit our energy, time and resources to the works of God. He is just, faithful, compassionate, and merciful and we must also replicate and exhibit the same nature. We must hallow his name and have reverential fear of him. We must refrain from detestable things God hates such as idol worship, bloodshed, sexual immorality, injustice, deceit, and all forms of lying that are abominable to him and his name.

Likewise, we must also love our neighbours as ourselves. The reasons amongst others why the world is so chaotic today, is because many people have no or little love of their neighbours. Christ died for us because of his love for us, yet no one is willing today to die for other people's "wills and needs." Most people today come up with wicked schemes such as wars, divisions, tribalism, corruption, bribery, injustice, violence, abuse, slavery, and all forms of human oppression to harm their neighbours.

The true love of our neighbours or others is to share the message of salvation with them. The word of God can not only convict people of their sins to repentance but also change their way of life without being critical or judgemental of them. We must also, where possible if we are blessed with material resources, share with people in need and who are not our close family members or friends. In the Bible a story is told of a good Samaritan, who looked after a Jew who was injured by the criminals on his way from Jerusalem to Jericho, even though the injured man's fellow Jews, including a priest, bypassed him when he was in need. The Samaritan became the true neighbour of the man who was beaten and injured by the criminals. He had to nurse the man's wounds and pay for the cost of his accommodation and food. Furthermore, he might have sacrificed his own life for the sake of the injured man by stopping on a dangerous road, and looking after his needs, an action for which he could have been killed by the criminals had they found him. His act is the true meaning of looking after our neighbours. We must replicate the same thing today as Christians to our neighbours.

SELF-RIGHTEOUSNESS

What is self-righteousness? It is a person's belief of being always right in what they think, speak, and do. It is inherent within human beings that they are right, and they want to be always right. But what people failed to understand is how do they conclude that they are right? What is the measurement of their righteousness? Many people base and measure their righteousness on their decision-making mechanism and the outcomes, such as reputation, education, status in the community, leadership position, wealth, personal moral values, family status, systems and procedures, ethical guidelines and code of conduct, rules, and regulations. These are some of the ways in which some people of the world justify themselves. Whether we justify ourselves through our own actions or we are justified by other people, none of those justifications qualifies us for the kingdom of God. None of our work will qualify us for heaven. In fact, what is called good by mankind is abominable to the Lord. God's justification of righteousness is totally different from the world.

The true justification of righteousness for us Christians comes from the justification of Christ by God. The righteousness of Christ to God became our righteousness. Christ obediently and willingly served God to the point of death to obtain the righteousness of God for us. Unless we come through Christ's justification to God, we will never see him. We have sinned and have fallen short of God's glory. None of us is righteous in our own eyes and our own ways. If we compare our own works to Christ's works for God, we will be convinced that Christ deserves the righteousness of God over our own righteousness for God.

Romans 3:-²¹ But now the righteousness of God apart from the law is revealed, being witnessed by the Law and the Prophets, ²² even the righteousness of God, through faith in Jesus Christ, to all and on all who believe. For there is no difference; ²³ *for all have sinned and fall short of the glory of God,* ²⁴ *being justified freely by His grace through the redemption that is in Christ Jesus,* ²⁵ *whom God set forth as a propitiation by His blood, through faith, to demonstrate His righteousness, because in His forbearance God had passed over the sins that were previously committed,* ²⁶ *to demonstrate at the present time His righteousness, that He might be just and the justifier of the one who has faith in Jesus.* NKJV.

Sin separates us from God and his righteousness. Sin was abolished on the cross by our Lord Jesus Christ to bring us back again to Godly righteousness we had lost through Adam's sin. The blood of Jesus is the blood of covenant between God and us, for us to qualify for God's righteousness. God only recognises the blood of Jesus Christ as the atonement for our sins. We are now justified by the righteousness of God by faith in what Christ has done for us on the cross. By faith we have the right to access our heavenly blessings through Christ from God. We need the help of our lord Jesus Christ and the Holy Spirit to see ourselves as sinners who cannot qualify for God's righteousness by our own ways and our own works. Godly righteousness is not a one-off thing, that we can obtain through repentance and baptism of the Holy Spirit, but rather a continuous process of living a sinless lifestyle until death. If we continue to commit sin and never repent of it, then we can easily be disqualified by it. St Paul warned us not to run like athletes that need to be disqualified, but rather like athletes that will qualify for a prize. Our prize is the righteousness and the salvation of our souls that need our continuous commitment to qualify for it.

MIND/BRAIN

The human mind is a part of the human soul. The human mind is composed of our thoughts, imaginations, and creativity. The human mind is divided into conscious and subconscious parts. The conscious part is where we receive the information, think, and reasoned over it, either to send it to the subconscious part if we agree with it, or reject it, if we don't agree with it. The subconscious part is where we store our deep held beliefs, norms, values, principles, and other human moral ethics. The entire human being, body, soul and spirit, are interconnected through the nerve systems within the human cells. What is happening in the soul for example is felt by both body and spirit. So, we speak of physical, mental and spiritual parts of us that make us complete beings.

Let me ask you this thought-provoking question; Where do our human thoughts come from? Well, I would love to hear how you would answer this question but let me give you the two sources of our thoughts. They come either from the information we receive into our bodies from the outside world using our five senses or from our spirit (through the help of Holy Spirit). This concept is discussed extensively in my other book; The human being as tripartite, body, soul and sprit. You can get yourself a copy of the book if you want to have more knowledge about this area.

Ephesians 1:17-19 That the God of our Lord Jesus Christ, the Father of glory, may give to you the spirit of wisdom and revelation in the knowledge of Him, the eyes of your understanding being enlightened; that you may know what is the hope of His calling, what are the riches of the glory of His inheritance in the saints, and what is the exceeding greatness of His power toward us who believe, according to the working of His mighty power. NKJV.

It is crystal clear in these verses that it is God who grants us his spirit to think the way we think. It is the Holy Spirit given to us by God, who oversees our thinking as Christians and non-Christians alike. The difference is that Christians will recognise the Holy Spirit and non-Christians will not because they have no experience with him. The Holy Spirit is referred to here as a spirit of wisdom, revelation, knowledge and understanding. It is the Holy Spirit who grants us the wisdom, revelation, knowledge and understanding of the things of God. But not only that, but he also reveals our own call or our purpose. It is he who gives us the reason and purpose for which we were created by God. Our thoughts, creativities and imagination come from him. We must make the Holy Spirit our friend instead of career professionals. The career professional will never give us the true purpose of our call and our existence. We must look inwardly to ourselves and within ourselves for the fountains of living waters. Our great purpose will always come from within us. For example, the systems of the world gave St Paul a justice career, and our Lord Jesus Christ gave him Apostleship. He was born with a calling of Apostleship, yet he never knew until it was revealed to him by Jesus Christ himself on the way to Damascus. The world gave St Paul a career he thought was the best, yet he never knew that the Apostleship career would make him known all over the world. God is the solo custodian of our thoughts and our true purposes. God has a true career for every single human.

It is critical to understand how our minds work in order to understand ourselves better, and the world around us. The way we think shapes our today and tomorrow. Good thoughts improve our lives and bad thoughts destroy our lives. If we refuse to allow God to lead us, then we can easily stumble with bad thoughts. The greatest tennis star and the humble servant of the highest God, Margaret Court, described our minds as computers programmed by things such as our own words, the words of others, the hurts of life, old habits and our senses and feelings. A computer is programmed by the raw data and information it receives into its process systems; it cannot produce anything without the programming. The same thing applies to our minds, they are programmed by thoughts and what is happening around us.

The factors and the conditioning of our minds comes either from God or from the world. If we are not born-again with the Holy Spirit actively working within us, whether we are Christians or not, we are programmed by the devil, world and our own flesh. The non-born-again person has a dead spirit that has no sensitivity to the things of God. Even the born-again Christians risked being dominated by thoughts of flesh, the devil and the world unless they are actively listening and obediently following the instructions and the directions of the Holy Spirit. Our minds must be transformed by the word of God. The word of God has all the capabilities to deprogram our minds from the worldly programming that has happened to us over many years of our lives. The word of God can transform our character, thoughts, words and actions. We as Christians no longer walk the way the world walks but the way Christ walks. We have now become children of light. In light there is no darkness. Our minds are now reprogrammed by the truth, knowledge, wisdom, understanding and revelation principles of God's kingdom. The kingdom of God is the kingdom of righteousness, peace, love, joy, mercy, kindness, faithfulness, justice, and self-control among others.

There is no vacuum; if our minds are not programmed by the word of God, then they can be programmed by the words of humans, which are also words of the devil. Our faith must not be based on things of this world but the things of heaven. All that there is in the world and in human beings are evil thoughts, adultery, bloodshed, sexual immorality, fornication, wickedness, deceit, foolishness, envy, blasphemy, pride, greed, corruption, jealousy, lying, and all other wicked schemes that we have been and will continue being programmed with on the inside. We have only two options; either we can choose to be programmed by good, or by evil. We can choose to lead a lifestyle that God wants us to lead or the lifestyle the devil wants us to lead. Our human minds are the target and the centre of this battle; we can choose who we give our minds to, to be programmed.

As Christians, our minds are the target of Satan, and we must be aware of this and take care of them. If Satan can easily capture our thoughts, then everything about us is all over. A dead brain to the things of God is a dead whole human being. The following are reasons why is this; the choices we make, the thoughts we have and the emotions that drive them are so critical to our lives. We must take control of our minds by bringing all thoughts and imagination under the obedience of Christ. We must pray to God continually to bless us with his thoughts and imagination to preach his word with power, authority, courage, boldness and confidence in the devil infested world. We must think and act the way our Lord Jesus Christ does. Before you do anything, pause for a moment and ask yourself this question; Will this decision I am making, please God? What does the Bible say about the action I am about to take? With these questions in mind, you can never go wrong in your decision-making. When we renew our minds daily with the word of God, we can love God and his thoughts. Although King David fell many times, he was a fanatic about God's thoughts, because he knew that his thoughts were not good enough for him to depend on and so he opted for God's thoughts and ways. Using God's thoughts and ways, David saw waves of successes in his leadership. We must also do the same if we are to succeed in our generation. Indeed, God looks upon the sons and daughters of mankind to bless with his thoughts and his ways, for them to succeed. Commit to God and he will commit to you. His thoughts and ways are far better than ours.

EMOTIONS

What is an emotion? It is a strong positive or negative feeling or attitude towards a certain thing or situation. The human emotions are parts of our human soul. The feelings, memories, attitudes, moods, and all other forms of human expression of emotions or reactions, constitute our emotions. Some examples of human emotions are happiness, sadness, anger, and fear. Our emotions are God-given purposely for us to express our state of being as human beings. Depending on the situation we find ourselves in, we can use our emotions to express ourselves to others and to the larger extent, to ourselves as well.

The subconscious mind is a home to our beliefs, attitudes, emotions, feelings, and memories, which drive our daily thinking. Our beliefs, feelings and attitudes are formed either through our five senses or deep down within our spirits-purpose, meaning and vision. The emotions drive our daily behaviours. You can see now how the whole human being is highly interconnected. What is happening within any of our three parts; body, soul and spirit will affect the other parts. The way you react to conditions or situations will determine how you behave. The way you react to events or happenings around you determine what kind of chemical the brain releases to your body. The brain can release healthy or toxic chemicals into our bodies based on our negative or positive reactions to the events happening around us. You can see how our thinking is critical to our life. As mentioned earlier, every part of our human body is interconnected through nerve systems that communicate with each other through neurons. The neurons are responsible for communicating information into and from our bodies, particularly our brains and heart.

Let me prove this to you in the context of stress or stressful situations or events you are facing or happening around you. Your body through the five senses receives the information about the stressful event and sends it to your brain- particularly conscious brain for reason and thinking. Your conscious brain sends the information into the subconscious brain for a response. Depending on the response from the subconscious brain through either emotions, feelings or beliefs, a positive or negative chemical can be released in response to the event. For example, the stressful event can cause our brains to release a chemical called cortisol, that prepares our bodies to respond either in fight or flight mode, at the expense of other parts of our bodies. Do this practical test to understand this better.

When you see or hear of stressful events try to see how your body responds to the information-physically, mentally, and emotionally. Pay attention particularly to your positive or negative response to the event and see how your body responds in its three parts. What emotions are you releasing in response to the event? What sensations are you feeling as your body is experiencing the event? Are your responses to the information angry or panicky? Is your heart beating more quickly? Are experiencing sweaty or cool hands, or are you-struggling to find the correct words? Here are additional experiences. When you are injured, your entire body feels pain, when you receive good news, your entire body responds in excitement and when you receive complements from people, your entire body feels good. What about when you receive insults and abuse? How does your body respond? You can answer it yourself. It looks like a simple exercise, yet it is important to your very existence on Earth. Well managed emotions mean a good life, and mismanaged emotions mean a bad life. I have taken my time to bring to your attention how critical your soul is, and particularly your emotions, to your daily life.

The wisdom of God warned us not to respond to information or events with our emotions but our spirits. God the Holy Spirit wants to manage our emotions and to a larger extent, our entire body if we are to succeed in this life against the devil. If we respond to events using our emotions every single time, we will be overwhelmed by negative emotions. Because of our sinful nature, we tend to respond to events negatively. When we do this, chemicals such as dopamine, and norepinephrine, and serotonin among others are released into our bodies. When these chemicals are released in excess into our bodies, they can cause damage to our bodies. Our daily thinking and emotions respond to them. We cannot stop thinking about our families, finances, businesses, jobs, investments, sports, promotions, reputation, politics, wars, violence, hatred, jealousy, injustice, and so much more. This is the nature of the world we live in, and we cannot stop thinking about these unless we are dead. God has given us the ability to think and to determine our own future through our thinking. The Bible is very clear that a person must plan, and God will direct their plans. So, if you have nothing planned to bring to God then God, can direct nothing.

We can never avoid thinking but we can avoid thinking negatively about the events happening to us and around us. Well, you may ask, Is it possible not to think negatively every time? Yes indeed, it is possible. You can choose to think positively or negatively every time you receive new information. As I mentioned earlier, if you respond using your emotions to every situation you are most likely going to respond negatively, particularly if it is bad news. How do you train your brain to respond positively to the negative news? Here is the Bible verse.

Philippians 4:6-9 Be anxious for nothing, but in everything by prayer and supplication, with thanksgiving, let your requests be made known to God; and the peace of God, which surpasses all understanding, will guard your hearts and minds through Christ Jesus. Finally, brethren, whatever things are true, whatever things are noble, whatever things are just, whatever things are pure, whatever things are lovely, whatever things are of good report, if there is any virtue and if there is anything praiseworthy--meditate on these things. The things which you learned and received and heard and saw in me, these do, and the God of peace will be with you. NKJV.

God wants us to train our minds to manage both good and bad through our spirit not our souls, and particularly our emotions. Although, I will discuss the spirit part of us in the next chapter, I will say this; our spirits are where the Spirit of God (Holy Spirit) communes with our spirits. Our spirits are also homes to our true meaning of life and purpose. They are the home of our wisdom, knowledge, understanding and deep revelations of things of life. That is why it is dangerous to respond to events with our emotions and not our spirits, where our true purposes of life are. When we respond using our emotions, then we rule out the true part of us which is our spirit.

Firstly, the starting point to our stress is anxiety. When we are anxious about what to eat, what to wear, where to live, who to marry, lack of job, sickness in our bodies, divorce, rebellious children, deception, corruption, greed, and all forms of human injustice, then we can easily get off track and the trajectory of our lives. These things have potential to not only cause anxiety, but stress and depression. St Paul warned us every time we are about to worry about things, then we should straight away report to God through prayer in order to have the peace of God that can calm our minds, as we seek wisdom from God to tackle them. After we have prayed, we know that God has heard us, and he will respond to our request. This will calm our spirits and our souls. So, every time you are about to worry, you need to start praying to God, instead of obsessing over these issues, which may make your situation worse, when you cannot find solutions to them.

Secondly, we must train our brains to think on good things and not the bad things frequently. St Paul again puts it very clearly that we must think on things which are true, noble, just, pure, lovely, whatever is of good report, praiseworthy, and virtuous; these are the things we must think about on daily basis (Philippians 4:8). There are many things stated here that we need to think about, and which may keep us wondering because they have not been explained in detail. Let me take for example things that are of good report that we need to think about. We receive many reports today in the world, which might be a doctor's report about our bad or good health, job performance, business earnings and profits, study results, and other forms of the things around our livelihoods. These reports have potential to cause us anxiety particularly when they are bad reports. For example, when you walked into the doctor's office, and he pronounces to you through a medical report that you are sick with cancer, and you are left with six months to live. How would you respond to this? The first thing is that you would be shocked and get worried for the rest of your life that is left according to the doctor. Will you leave that doctor's office and consult with another who has seen better rates of cancer survival? Then you would have two opinions about your situation. Now you have two reports to think about, whether to stick with first doctor's report or the second doctor's report about your sickness. One is positive and one is negative. The positive news is that you can survive the cancer like other previous patients and the negative news is that cancer can kill you like its previous victims. Besides that, the reality of the disease kicks in and you are feeling pains everywhere in your body and the fear of death begins to creep into your mind saying to you, it is all over for you, and you will die. Your brain now begin to slip into negative thinking, and you cannot recover from it, if you have no hope in God. Alternatively, you can choose to let your brain think about the survivors of the cancer, and your brain speaks to you that you can also survive it. Additionally, as well, the word of God if you are a believer says, that you are already healed by the stripes of our Lord Jesus Christ. Watch this; before you were born and before you even got sick, Christ died for you, and all your sicknesses were healed. This is the advantage of the mind Christians have over non-Christians in managing their awful situations. Now practically you can choose to think of the doctor's bad report of your sickness, corresponding with the symptoms in your body or with the good report of your healing in the Bible. This is what St Paul referred as things of good report that we must think about continuously.

Until recently, when Lord delivered me from the spirit of anger, I was a victim of anger for a long time due to my emotional responses to many events around me. Let me tell you my own-story of anger and taking offence. In as much as our emotion of anger is good, it cannot be applied or used unreasonably, randomly and in unnecessary ways. There are certain things that are worth our fight, but not all things. We must be angry when it is fitting and reasonable. God himself has not banned us from getting angry but we must not let the sun go down while we are still angry either with ourselves or others, or else it will bring destruction. Let me admit I was an angry man with my emotions, and it was not under my control when I got angry. When I was angry it was very hard for me to calm down or for someone else to calm me down. I was very quick to get offended or get angry. When this happened, it was very hard for people around me not to get hurt either with my words or physical violence. I still remember vividly on Christmas day in 2002, in Kakuma Refuge Camp, Kenya, when I fought with my cousin. Our fight on Saturday evening extended to Sunday, Christmas day. On that Sunday morning I dressed up to go to church and immediately came back from the church to undressed and to resume the fight. I came back from church that day and searched for my cousin to resume the fight. I found him at my other cousin's house. He smiled at me, signalling that the fight is over, but I couldn't accept this. I told him to get up so that we could continue to fight. He told me he was not ready to fight. I kept saying Get up so that we can fight, and as I moved closer to him, I released a fist and I hit him on his face. He stood up and told me, I am not fighting you although you have hit me on the head with your fist. People who were present intervened and we were separated, and I went back to my house. While in my own house, I thought through my actions, and I was embarrassed by them, but my pride could not allow me to go back to him and apologise for my awful actions. Although there are many other incidents where I got offended and got into a fight with people, I can remember this as the worst of all my fights. I thought back then that a fight will discipline a person not to offend, undermine, blackmail, or belittle me next time. I was wrong; you cannot discipline another a human being through a fight.

We can easily fall into the trap of the devil when we respond to events using our emotions instead of our spirits. I never knew that the uncontrollable anger was the work of the devil until God revealed it to me recently. It is important to point out that the demonic spirits of anger and offence work together in order to get us to be always violent. If there is a part of our soul that is easily subject to demonic influence and manipulation, then it is our emotions. That is why St Paul said, never give place to the devil through anger. When we are angry, we are subject to demonic attacks. It causes more harm than good. Think what can happen when you are angry; you can break things around you, utter insults and abuse at your opponents including those shameful words you wouldn't say when you were sober, and the worst-case scenario is that you hit someone, and you may kill them. Uncontrollable anger is dangerous.

Ephesians 4:26-27 "Be angry, and do not sin": do not let the sun go down on your wrath, nor give place to the devil. NKJV.

The Bible is very clear; being angry is not sinning. Sinning comes in when we are angry continuously until we go to bed. What happens when we go to bed angry? I don't know about you, but I cannot sleep while my emotions are still highly charged. So, what do we do while in bed? We think about revenge attacks on our opponents who have wronged us. While we think about the revenge, our thoughts can be subject to demonic influence and can easily be altered by the devil because there are no people around us to calm us down or to give us alternative advice. If we choose revenge, then we give place to the devil. While we are thinking about revenge strategies all we are filled with is bitterness, anger, wrath and all forms of malice against our opponents. All of these are fertile grounds of evil and you can easily be trapped. By doing this, you give ground to the devil.

More importantly when we allow our emotions to be used or influenced by the devil and our sinful nature, this can grieve the Holy Spirit. The Spirit of God hates lewdness, filthiness, insults and abuse, lying, anger, wrath and all forms of evil communication that comes out of our mouths. Remember God is Holy, and our unholy nature and conduct can either lead him to be silent or withdraw from us. At the time we are angry, this is the time we must seek his counsel on the matter instead of taking it into our own hands. It is dangerous to lose the seal of our salvation if we are born-again Christians. He is also the lord of our peace, love, and joy. If we want to be happy almost every day and to keep anger at bay, we must commit to his counsel daily. We must allow the word of God to take root inside us and it will bring under control every uncontrollable part of our soul including our emotions. When we commit to the guiding of the Holy Spirit, he can control what we speak, what we think and what we store within our own hearts. It a common practice for the people of the world to control their thoughts, words and actions through drinking of alcohol, drugs, cigarettes and sex instead of the Holy Spirit, who can remove difficult situations from our lives, permanently and completely. No matter what difficult situation you may find yourself in, there is nothing the Holy Spirit cannot do within you. If you have the problems of anger, offence, bad attitudes, and moods that control your emotions, then commit to the Spirit of God today. If God can deliver me from the spirit of anger, then no doubt, he will do it for you.

8

YOUR SPIRIT; THE COMMMUNICATION MEANS WITH THE HOLY SPIRIT IN YOU

GOD COMMUNICATES WITH YOU THROUGH YOUR HUMAN SPIRIT

HUMAN SPIRIT/HEART

Our human spirits were created by God purposely for communication with him. Our spirits are where the spirit of God communes with us. It is our spirits that can be born-again with the spirit of God. It is our spirits which relate with the spirit of God giving us deep revelations of God's knowledge. It is within our spirits that the Holy Spirit moves and convicts us of sins. The spirit enables us to transcend our abilities, limitations, and circumstances as we are regenerated or reborn, indwelt by the Holy Spirit. The spirit is the element in humanity that gives us the ability to have an intimate relationship with God. Whenever the word" spirit" is used, it refers to the immortal part of humanity that "connects" with God, who Himself is spirit (John 4:24). The Human spirit/heart is the immortal part of the human being that does not die, and which was created in the image of God. We know God is a spirit and so as human beings, we are spirits. From the very beginning of the Bible, we can see that God made us with his Godly Spirit (human spirit). The human spirit (which is true us) was created out of God's spirit. Genesis 2:7 says, "Jehovah God formed man from the dust of the ground and breathed into his nostrils the breath of life, and man became a living soul." The human spirit in this verse can be seen here as we break down the body into three parts: body, soul and spirit. "The dust of the ground" becomes the physical body, "A living soul" is your soul, which is your psychological part of you, your mind, your emotions, and your will. "The breath of life" is your human spirit. This is clearly stated and backed up by the book of Proverbs 20:27, "The spirit of man is the lamp of Jehovah."

We can never know the things of God unless we allow the Spirit of God (the Holy Spirit) to come and live inside of us and to commune with our Spirits. Just as the spirit of man can only understand the things of man, it also applies that we cannot understand the things of God, unless the Spirit of God enables us to do so. It is difficult to understand another human being unless they have spoken to us about themselves. We also cannot understand God unless God has chosen to speak to us. The Bible is very clear, if you cannot understand the things of the world, how can you understand the things of heaven? Unless we allow the spirit of our lord Jesus Christ to come and live inside of us, we cannot understand the things of heaven. The things of heaven are spiritually known and spiritually discerned. You cannot know them by your body and soul unless your spirit is involved and active.

I Corinthians 2:9-16- But as it is written: "Eye has not seen, nor ear heard, Nor have entered into the heart of man The things which God has prepared for those who love Him." But God has revealed them to us through His Spirit. For the Spirit searches all things, yes, the deep things of God. For what man knows the things of a man except the spirit of the man which is in him? Even so no one knows the things of God except the Spirit of God. Now we have received, not the spirit of the world, but the Spirit who is from God, that we might know the things that have been freely given to us by God. These things we also speak, not in words which man's wisdom teaches but which the Holy Spirit teaches, comparing spiritual things with spiritual. But the natural man does not receive the things of the Spirit of God, for they are foolishness to him; nor can he know them, because they are spiritually discerned. But he who is spiritual judges all things, yet he himself is rightly judged by no one. For "who has known the mind of the Lord that he may instruct Him?" But we have the mind of Christ. NKJV.

In as much as these verses are loaded with a lot of information, I must first point out the fact that the things of God are only known to us through the spirit of God who lives in us. But not only that, these things must be made known to us through the Spirit of God. Things that have been freely given to us by God, are our own things. To me these are the most encouraging and appealing Bible verses to we who love God. According to these verses there are things God has given us, that we must know, hear, see and must enter our spirit through the help of the Holy Spirit. If you love God, then this is for you and if you will believe and thereafter love God, then this will be also for you. There are things in heaven for us that we must receive through the Holy Spirit. But this can only happen when we have allowed the spirit of God to live inside us for him to communicate them to us. You may ask what are these things? The good examples of these things are long life, power, riches, wisdom, understanding, glory, grace, righteousness, love, peace, joy, honour, truth, salvation, discernment, fear of God, word of God, blood of Jesus Christ and the list can be endless. If we want to know the things of God, then we must allow the Holy Spirit to live inside us to reveal these deep things of God to us.

Furthermore, it is also stated in **I Corinthians 2:11a "For what man knows the things of a man except the spirit of man which is in him?"** In the ideal world, no man or woman knows the things of other man or woman, except that man and woman only. Although we may attempt to know the things or the secrets of other people through their thoughts, words, and conduct, we may not know them all. There are deep secrets of people that we may not know until they die or unless they have chosen to tell us. Deep inside every human being lies their beliefs, values, desires, will, and other things of this world that are not known to people. No matter how you get closer to the person you may not know about them at all. There are things people may be ashamed of sharing with us, or there may be secret things people have been successful in, and they fear if they share them with us then they may be overtaken in their success.

SENDING: PRAYER

Prayer is an important means of communication with God. Many people take prayer lightly, yet it is the only way we can communicate with God. If we cannot pray, then we are not in communication with God. In fact, the responsibility for us to communicate with God has been squarely put on us. If we cannot make a move to pray, then we must not expect God to do anything for us. Yes, indeed there are some things God can sometimes do unilaterally in our lives, but if we want continuous ongoing relationship with him, then we can develop that through prayer. Think about any other close relationship you have with people, particularly your family members, friends, and colleagues; can you maintain them without continuous communication? There is no way you can have a close relationship with important people in your life if you don't talk to them. The same thing applies to our relationship with God. There is no way we can maintain it without communicating to him. The Bible puts the onus on us to start the communication.

Matthew 7:7-"Ask, and it will be given to you; seek, and you will find; knock, and it will be opened to you. NJKV.

The starting point is on us; "ask," "How do we ask? It is through prayer. Whatever we want God to do for us it must be through prayer. If only way we can have things from God, is through prayer, then God can answer prayers in return. So, we put our request through, and God can answer in return. **Matthew 7:8 "For everyone who asks receives."** Think about it, the only way we can receive from God is by asking. Now this verse tells you the importance of your prayers. It does not matter who we are; whether Jew or Gentile, high or low, rich or poor, master or servant, educated or uneducated, young or old, all are invited to the throne of God by faith to receive blessings from him. I must emphasise this; God is not a respecter of man. If you cannot humbly come before his throne by faith to seek his help, then you cannot receive from him. Reflect on your times when you were very young and how you had depended on your parents to provide for you. How many times did you ask for their help? How many times did they provide for you when you had asked? Parents love those children who ask them things over those who don't, or those who takes things illegally. Prayer is so important to God, and that is why he came to the Earth to teach us how to pray. God is looking for those who would pray so that he can release their blessings. But not only that, but he is also seeking those who will make prayer part of their lives so that they can pray on behalf of others.

That aside, it is one thing to pray, but it is another thing to pray according to the "Will" of God. Please don't get me wrong, it is a good starting point if you can pray, but to pray right, we need the help of God. There was something wrong with our prayers, that's why God came to correct it. Jews did pray, but they didn't know how to pray right. Gentiles did pray but they had prayed to the wrong gods (Demons and Satan). Although, Jews did pray to the right God, their prayers were full of glorious vain and repetitive words that didn't get answered by God. That is how flawed our prayer life was on Earth without God's knowledge. Now that we have the indwelling of the Holy Spirit within us, we can pray rightful prayers according to the "Will" of God. When we pray, it must be according to the "will" of God for us or for those we are praying on their behalf. Before we pray about anything we must pause for a moment and think about what we are about to ask God, whether it is within his "will" for himself, us and others. Three things are needed to be considered before we pray. Ask yourself these questions; Is what I am about to ask in prayer pleasing to God, and can he answer me positively? Is something I am about to ask God, for my personal selfish gain or is it something justifiable for me to have? Is the person I am about to pray for, willing that I pray on his behalf? Besides the help of the Holy Spirit, these questions I believed will help you, in a rightful way of directing your prayers to God. Unless we come humbly before his throne, we cannot have our prayers answered. Unless we pray according to his "will" we cannot have our prayers answered. So, two things are critical for our prayer life; "humility" and the "Will" of God. We must always have these at out fingertips. God is willing to give us what we want but he will not if he knows that it is something that is going to destroy us. For example, if a drunkard asked God, through a prayer to blessed them with money to drink, will God answer such a prayer? I am not victimising drunkards here because we are all sinners. All I am saying, is that God can reject our prayers sometimes for our own good. If you are an adulterer and you asked God through prayer to give you a wife, will God answer such prayer? When he knows that you are going to cheat on her. In addition, we cannot pray right without the help of the Holy Spirit. It is with the help of the Holy Spirit that our prayers can be channelled right.

Romans 8:26-27 Likewise the Spirit also helps in our weaknesses. For we do not know what we should pray for as we ought, but the Spirit Himself makes intercession for us with groanings which cannot be uttered. Now He who searches the hearts knows what the mind of the Spirit is, because He makes intercession for the saints according to the will of God. **NKJV.**

In times of our needs and particularly when we are in a desperate situation of which we need God to answer our prayers, the Holy Spirit is there to help us pray right. At our weakest points of desperation such as when we are sick, stressed, depressed, disappointed, sad, angry and with no hope, the Holy Spirit becomes the source of our strength. It is not good enough to pray to God in our own ways and our own thinking. Think about it. These are the words of the man most experienced in the things of God, St Paul. The greatest example for him, was when he was so desperate for healing in his body. Imagine what he called "the thorn in the flesh", a messenger of Satan given to him to buffet him lest he should exalt himself above and beyond measure. He was so desperate for healing, yet God would not heal him, but gave him sufficient grace to protect him in his weakness. This proves again to us that everything we pray for must fall within God's "Will" for our lives. The "Will" of God was that St Paul wouldn't be healed, but live with the thorn in the flesh, while not being harmed by it. Because he had the full protection of God with him. At the weakest stage of St Paul, the Holy Spirit was there praying for him.

The Holy Spirit teaches us how to pray rightful prayers to God and according to his "Will." He helps us overcome our fears and discouragements that may affect the wording of our prayers, by taking over and praying on our behalf. There are words that the Holy Spirit may speak through our prayers that we may not know, that may make our prayers be heard by God. With the help of the Holy Spirit, our "Will" can be easily aligned to the "Will" of God during our prayers. The Holy Spirit quickly searches our hearts and minds to bring our desires and needs to the "Will" of God during our prayers.

FASTING

Although prayer is the habitual thing that we need to conduct daily, fasting is the next level up. Prayer is the "cake" and fasting is the "icing" on the cake. For those in the Western culture, it would be very unusual to have cake without iced on top. I may not have a deeper meaning of what the icing does to the cake or the importance of it on the cake, but my little understanding is that it adds taste and attractiveness to the cake. The same thing applies to the prayer and fasting. Fasting adds taste and attractiveness to our prayers. There must be moments in our lives where we deny ourselves attractive things of this world and seek God in sorrow due to the situation we are in or some of our family members are in or when we are about to make the important decisions of our lives. For example, where to live as a family, job to do, contracts to sign, people to employ or sack, projects to start, friends to make, amongst others. We may also fast when we are sick or one of our family members is sick, when natural disasters hit our region or country, when there is confusion and division among the people in our communities, when war is ravaging our country, when there is rampant corruption, bloodshed, sexual immorality and injustice in both church and government. We live in a fallen world and there are many reasons, why we may seek God, in sorrow and disappointment always, through fasting. It is in this confusion and turbulence in the world around us that we run to God, to seek answers and solutions to our problems. Our Lord Jesus Christ has not hidden from us that in this world we shall have troubles, but even if so, we must be happy because he has overcome the world. His victory over the world is one of the reasons, we must seek him in fasting to direct us on how to overcome what is troubling us. In fact, this is not an isolated claim. He invited us to come to him if we are "heavy laden, and burdened. The problems of this world are the burdens our Lord is talking about.

Matthew 11:28-30- 28 Come to Me, all you who labour and are heavy laden, and I will give you rest. Take My yoke upon you and learn from Me, for I am gentle and lowly in heart, and you will find rest for your souls. For My yoke is easy and My burden is light." NKJV.

When we fast, we must get our motives and objectives of fasting right, before we can come to God, to seek his direction and guidance. Our intention for fasting must be pure and within God's "Will." Don't get me wrong it is good to fast and indeed I do appreciate the fact that you do fast. It is a good starting point to fast. But if you want to see many breakthroughs and many victories then you must get your motives and objectives right with God. If you do go into fasting with objectives and motives that are outside God's "will," then he will either hold your request until you get it right or he will reject your request straight away. There are standards needed in fasting so that God can answer us quickly and powerfully, and the Prophet Isaiah has described them very well for us.

Isaiah 58:3-7 'Why have we fasted,' they say, 'and You have not seen? Why have we afflicted our souls, and You take no notice?' "In fact, in the day of your fast you find pleasure, And exploit all your laborers. Indeed you fast for strife and debate, And to strike with the fist of wickedness. You will not fast as you do this day, To make your voice heard on high. Is it a fast that I have chosen, A day for a man to afflict his soul? Is it to bow down his head like a bulrush, And to spread out sackcloth and ashes? Would you call this a fast, And an acceptable day to the Lord? "Is this not the fast that I have chosen: To loose the bonds of wickedness, To undo the heavy burdens, To let the oppressed go free, And that you break every yoke? Is it not to share your bread with the hungry, And that you bring to your house the poor who are cast out; When you see the naked, that you cover him, And not hide yourself from your own flesh? NKJV.

This is exactly what I was saying in the above paragraph. The Israelites were fasting, yet they never saw breakthroughs in their fasting. What was the reason they never got their breakthroughs from God through their fasting? Well, they never got their objectives and motives of their fasts right. The problem was never on God's side – the problems were on their side. While they were fasting, they were committing sins amongst themselves. They were busy fighting amongst themselves, quarrelling, debating, gossiping, lying, denying themselves food and drinks, shelter, clothes, and oppressing the widows and the poor in their communities. The desired outcomes of their fasting that they had sought God for, were hindered by their own sins. What does this tell you now? I don't about you, but it looks like it is a waste of time to come to God in fasting while still sinning. The prophet Isaiah has given us a good model to follow before we commit ourselves to fasting. It is crystal clear that fasting should never be about denying yourself food and drinks for certain times, it should not be about putting on a sad face and wearing sackcloth and crying to God while sinning. It is abundantly clear here that the problems we are seeking God for through fasting, are of our own making. By sinning we are attracting the devil to ourselves and our communities. The devil is the lord over sin, and those who commit sin will attract the demons to possess them and continue to do so. At this point it will be almost impossible for a person or community to get rid of the devil and his demons without the help of God. Satan has power that outmatches the power of human beings without God.

At this point when we seek God through fasting, we would have completely freed ourselves from sins and cried out in repentance for God's intervention. When we cry out to God in fasting to fix our problems, we must share our resources with the widows, orphans, and the poor members of the community. Doing this creates good ground for God to answer and provide the solutions to our problems. Fasting is so critical for our Christian faith, as it has the potential to give us almost everything we need from God, and we must get it right. I say this with great confidence because I am a beneficiary of fasting. Most of my victories come when I have fasted, and I thank the living God for that. I know the power of fasting. That is why I have taken time to explain it, in order to get it right. The Devil and his demons will never give an inch of your freedom to you until you begin to back your prayers with fasting. I thank the living God that he set my finances free from the devourer, my sleep from familiar spirits, my emotions from the spirit of anger and my eyes from the spirits of lust. The list goes on of what the living God has delivered me from. All these deliverances were achieved through fasting and continuous prayers.

So, when I talk, I know exactly what I am talking about. I now sleep like a child without demonic visitations at night. I can now distinguish between a demonic dreams and God dreams. I can therefore unequivocally say that fasting is the way to go if you want to see your life change for the better if not forever. But remember always we must get it right.

There are many methods of fasting you can choose from. Firstly, the dry fast. This is where you deny yourself food and drink. The vegetable fast is where you eat fruits and vegetable only. And there are social fasts including, but not limited to, Facebook, football, and TV. Based on your health conditions and doctor's advice, fasting can range from one day to forty days. I must emphasise, based on the scientific community's advice, it must not go beyond forty days as your body may begin to shut down completely and may not recover from such a fast. We have seen many people dying from hunger strikes that go beyond forty days. I have personally done all these fasts – some with food and drink and some without food and drink. So, it must be with complete preparation from your side, and with your doctor's advice if you want to do one. I must confess that I have not yet done forty days without food and drink, but one day God willing, I may do it.

Like I said before when you deny yourself food and drink, you are not to sit and do nothing. These are moments where you seek God with your full attention. Because food and drink, social media, movies, sports, games, social gatherings, TV, and phone calls have potential to distract us from seeking God fully during our fast. If we cannot stop them completely then we must look at other ways of avoiding them. When you dedicate this time to God, you must study the Bible and meditate on it, commit to prayer, praise and worship, listening to sermons and preaching by great men and women of God, visit the sick in the hospital and prisoners in the prison, and your other daily activities connected to the service of God must continue including preaching the word if you are a preacher.

You must also prepare for opposition from Satanic powers because the devil knows where your power lies, and he must resist it by all means possible. I am not saying this to scare you, but to make you prepare, in case that happens. People are different and demonic resistance can differ from person to person. I say this from my own experiences over years, that it is during fasting that I get heavy demonic attacks. It is either before or during the fasting that you can get attacks. Perhaps it is not me alone who gets these attacks during fasting. Our Lord Jesus Christ came under attack immediately when just concluded his fasting. We are vulnerable during these times of fasting because we are exhausted and hungry for food and drink. These times we are most vulnerable and can come under the heavy attack by the devil to defeat us. Because Satan knows God can reward faithful fasting that is done according to God's "Will."

Fasting is a "rite of passage" for every Christian who has things of God at heart. Fasting is something that we must do in this life, if we are to see successes in what we do for the kingdom of heaven. Not only does fasting disciplined us to lead a better Christian life, but also, we have an enemy that is constantly following us looking for opportunities to attacks us – not only to shame us but to destroy us completely. In addition to that it is also a demand by God that we fast. Our Lord Jesus Christ, was asked by John's disciples, "'Why do we and the Pharisees fast often, but your disciples do not fast?' He answered, 'Can the friends of the bridegroom mourn as long as the bridegroom is with them?" continuing, "But the day will come when the bridegroom will be taken away from them, and then they will fast." Furthermore, when he was fasting, he was tempted by Satan to turn the stones into bread, and he answered, "Man should not live by bread alone, but by every word that proceeds from the mouth of God." (Matthew 4:4). When we have God's purpose and God's call over our lives, there is a resistance from the devil, and we can never win without God on our side as Christians. In fact, it is for our own good that we must fast. There was no need for the disciples of our Jesus Christ to fast while he was there with them. He was the shield and protector from the devil. In fact, he had to pray for them after the enemy's attack while he was there with them. For example, the devil asked Jesus to sieve Peter like wheat, but Jesus prayed for him that his faith should not fail while undergoing that testing (Luke 22:31). But as soon as he left them for heaven they came under heavy attack from the Pharisees and they were hiding in houses, some were scattered across nations and some were even killed such as Stephen, James and so many others. Now there was need for them to seek God in prayer and fasting for their protection as they preached the word to the nations. The same thing applies to us today. We must seek God in prayer and fasting for his guidance, protection, provision, worship, justice, righteousness, truth, salvation, words, voice, healing, dreams and visions and more importantly about the future.

STUDYING THE BIBLE

Meditate on the Bible Day and night and your revelation will be developed. The Bible is the true word of God. Part of it was written by God himself (the ten commandments), and other parts were written by men and women filled with the Holy Spirit. There is no other book on Earth that talks about the root, origin and creation of all things including mankind, apart from the Bible. There is no other book on Earth which talks about the past, present and the future events than the Bible. There is no other book on Earth which talks about the existence of the spiritual world apart from the Bible. More importantly no book on Earth which talks about mankind's origin, way of life, and life after death than the Bible. There is no book on Earth that answers difficult questions and provides solutions to and about the human sufferings and its causes, apart from the Bible. The Bible has true answers to our difficult questions of life including your own and you deserve to meditate on it day and night. The Bible is a constitution of God, given to us for our lives. It was written purposely for every single human being who exist on Earth, as it points us back to our creator (God).

The question you would ask now is what does the word meditate mean? Meditate means think over. Thinking over something means to have deep and calm thoughts about it. Think about the origin, purpose and meaning of something. When you meditate on the Bible you are thinking about every single word in the sentence, paragraph, page and the book. Look at how it progresses and how it gets interesting as you meditate on the word. This begs the question of the bigger picture; what is the message of the Bible for us? What is the meaning of its words, sentences and paragraphs communicating to us? As people are being led by the Holy Spirit, there are many methods people come up with to study the Bible. The few among them are maps, encyclopedia, dictionaries, Bible commentaries, sermons and teachings by great men and women of God, books, websites, online videos, peer reviewed scholarly articles written by great men and women of God, and other means available to them. My own personal favourite among these are Bible commentaries, dictionaries, and peer reviewed articles. My other ways are five-Ws and one H. Five Ws and one H stand for who, what, where, when why and how. Since my school days I have been using these five Ws and one H, for my studies. Obviously, these are human means and ways of studying the Bible, but the best teacher is the Holy Spirit, who inspired the Bible.

The onus is on you and me to ask, seek and knock on the door of heaven (Matthew 7:7). Apart from the few that God comes after when they have veered off from their call and God's assignment for them, we have the responsibility to ask, seek and knock on the door of heaven. Paul was among this group who had veered away from their call and God had to intervene to reined him back in. He had an assignment from God to bring the Gentiles back to God. This was his assignment from birth, yet he did not discover it until God intervened in a dramatic way, on Paul's way to Damascus to persecute Christians, through an audible voice. His zeal to kill Christians was so dangerous that God had to intervene to stop it. St Paul had crossed the line, and God had to intervene. Perhaps it is okay to reject God, but it is never okay to kill those who have accepted their call from God. This is also a warning for everyone who rejects God today; never to persecute the children of God or else they will see God in action fighting the enemies of his children. It is not St Paul, alone. Many of us today have God's calls over our lives, yet we don't ask, seek and knock at his door for him to reveal them to us. That aside, let us go back to our main topic of discussion. While we meditate on the scriptures the Holy Spirit will be right there to assist us in asking (prayer), seeking (meditation – finding the right information and the right way), knocking (now you access heaven by faith). These sound like one gigantic step but there are three gigantic steps. For those who are hungry for the things of God these three steps must be adhered to and followed if we are to have access to the kingdom of heaven. We must be constantly asking God in prayer; we must be constantly seeking the right information and the ways to heaven and finally we must have faith to access the door of heaven. The Holy Spirit is so critical in helping us through these steps once the hunger and the thirst for the things of God is seen by him. Remember he is already inside us and all we must do is allow him to officially operate within us.

The deep revelations of the things of God will take off if we allow the Holy Spirit to help us meditate on the word. In the words of the great man of God, Dr Myles Munroe, "the Bible is like an onion, it has many layers that needs to be peeled off in order to have full understanding of it." And he is absolutely right. Even in the worldly context, words have surface and deeper meanings and context that make them difficult to be understood easily. For example, look at the word "right" I have used in the above sentence. "Right" has two meanings; the entitlement to things, and to be correct in what you are doing or saying. Words also have context, what do I mean by what I say, and what does what I say mean? You see how words can get complicated, if the right context is not applied. Interpretation of words is another thing. What do words mean to me individually and to other people? What am I trying to communicate to you here? It is a fact that the Bible is a complicated book that needs help and interpretation of the Holy Spirit. This is not meant to scare you away from studying the Bible, but never treat it lightly if you want to know the deep things of God. Deep things of God are revealed to us by the Holy Spirit. Let me prove this to you with my own example of taking scriptures literally with their surface meaning. **Mark 12:38 40. Then He said to them in His teaching, "Beware of the scribes, who desire to go around in long robes, love greetings in the marketplaces, the best seats in the synagogues, and the best places at feasts, who devour widows' houses, and for a pretense make long prayers. These will receive greater condemnation." NKJV.**

I will not interpret the whole verse but only verse 40, part a, "who devour widows' houses." Let me ask you this question and see how you will respond to it; Who are the widows our Lord Jesus Christ is talking about here? Your response to this question will not be far from mine. I used to talk or interpret this word "widow" in a surface and a literal meaning, as a woman whose husband is dead. To me it was clear, and I didn't have to seek the interpretation of the Holy Spirit until he told me otherwise. My recent restudies of this verse with the Holy Spirit has helped. Yes, indeed widow in the usual interpretation means a woman whose husband is dead. That is not what the word "widow" means in the heavenly context and meaning. Widow means a person who has no God in his life or people who have no God in their lives. This is the true interpretation of the word by the Holy Spirit, and I had to agree with his interpretation. This is also backed up Christ when he referred to himself has the bridegroom to the bride. We are the brides (the Church of God) and Christ is our husband. *2 Corinthians 11:2 For I am jealous for you with godly jealousy. For I have betrothed you to one husband, that I may present you as a chaste virgin to Christ. NKJV.*

Plus, many other Bible verses I can use to back up this interpretation of the Holy Spirit such as the parable of the wedding feast and the parable of the ten virgins among others. Let us go back to further explanation of the widow in order to have full understanding of what it means in the language and the context of heaven. Widow means a person without God or people without God. Why do they not have God? Because they have been devoured by religious leaders who represent them to God. Before the Holy Spirit came, people who believed in God were represented by the religious leaders, particularly the priests and the Levites. For example, priests were the only sources from whom the word of God could be heard and executed. Right from our Father of faith Abraham, Moses, Elijah, Isaiah, Jeremiah, John the Baptist and our Lord Jesus Christ, the word of God was channelled through them to the people. God spoke to the people of Israel through these great men of God and partly to us now, because we have the Holy Spirit. These people had the responsibility to teach people the ways, truth, and doctrines of God. By the time John the Baptist and our Lord Jesus Christ came onto the scene, there were other religious groups such as the Pharisees, scribes and

Sadducees who had established themselves as the representatives of God to the people of Israel and the entire world. It was only through this group of religious leaders that the word of God can be heard and interpreted. These religious groups would not allow anybody outside them to interpret or preach the word of God to people. They were the only channel to God. But here is the dangerous part of these groups. They were not able to hear from God, yet they represented God in the eyes of people. They made people widows by denying them their God. Apart from the Bible there was no other means they would allow people to access God, such as dreams and visions, voices, prophecy, and word of knowledge from God to the people. They reduced hearing from God to the Bible only. But as if this was not enough, they also misrepresented and misinterpreted the scriptures. By the time Christ came to the scene they were no longer believing in life after death, they were no longer mindful about sins in the flesh, or turning the house of God into the dens of thieves (selling and buying in it), collecting tithes and denying justice to the people of Israel, praying and fasting that did not have response from God, and more importantly denying people access to God. These groups had turned the ways of God to the ways of hell on Earth.

We study the Bible to develop our faith. Faith comes by hearing, and hearing by the word of God (Romans 10:17). If you want your faith to develop to the next level, then you must be committed to hearing the word of God. Because words have power to convince us but to also make us believe in them. In life you will have your favourite speakers whom you love dearly, and when they speak, their words enter deep into your heart. Sometimes it gets to a point that you cannot live without their words. Words of others have power to transform our own thoughts, actions, words and character. When the word of God is preached by those who are anointed by the Holy Spirit, it becomes completely different from those of ordinary preachers. The great men and women anointed by God have deeper understanding of scriptures, and while preaching the gospel, their words will sink into our hearts. The word of God is called a good news gospel because it can change your thinking to become a believer in the Messiah. The day you are convinced and believed in the word, that is the day it becomes good news to you. The moment you believe the word, that is the moment your faith develops.

God over the years has anointed and ordained great preachers of his word – ministers, apostles, priests, Evangelists to preach the word to people in order to develop their faith. It is a sincere wish of God that every man and woman be saved and so it is his responsibility to connect you with his anointed servants. There is no way you cannot believe in the word, when it is preached through the help of the Holy Spirit and fire. In addition, these great men and women preach the word with orders and instruction from God. They have the permission, mission and vision from our Lord Jesus Christ to preach the word. For the word preached through the permission of our Lord Jesus Christ and with the help of the Holy Spirit will convict us of our sins to believe in God. When the right doctrine of the word is taught, the word can change our thinking to believe that God is the one speaking to us directly through his servants. So, your faith will come by hearing, and hearing through the preachers of the word.

Besides that, I must put emphasis on hearing that word. Just as studying and meditating on the word is our responsibility, it is also our responsibility to seek out the great preachers of the word who are filled with the Holy Spirit, for us to develop our faith. It is when we are hungry and thirsty for the word that God can easily connect us to these preachers. It is important to note that it is God, who can enable us to hear his word. The Bible says" hearing, they do not hear." Which means even if you would have gone into the churches of these great men of God and heard the word from them, you may not still have heard the word. You may ask why this is? Because you may still be lacking faith to believe the word. The problem is not always with God, but with us as human beings. People who have hearts of stone have difficulty hearing the word. People who believe there is no God have difficulty hearing the word of God. People who believed in worldly religions and their traditions have difficulty believing the word of God. People who are ignorant about the word have difficulty hearing the word.

Your knowledge, wisdom, and understanding about God will increase when you study the Bible. The three words knowledge, wisdom and understanding seem alike yet they are totally different. Here is my simple definition of them; knowledge is the information, data, truth, facts, principles and examples you have about things or people. Wisdom is the application of the knowledge to help you make good decisions or judgement. Understanding is having a clear picture of what you want to do with the information, to achieve a certain outcome. So far with the definition of these words, what have you realised? Their meanings and definitions are totally different, yet they are interdependent in their use and application. If you have knowledge and lack both wisdom and understanding of certain things or people, then that knowledge is useless. If you have wisdom and understanding about things or people and lack knowledge about them, then it is still useless. That is why God gives them together to his children. A well-equipped child of God will have knowledge, wisdom and understanding of the Bible.

If you are a teacher, evangelist, apostle and prophet of the Bible, then you must have knowledge, wisdom and understanding of the word. In the ideal world setting, you cannot be a teacher without training, knowledge, wisdom and understanding of the curriculum and the teachable topics in it. The same thing applies to the teacher of the word; you cannot be a teacher without knowledge, wisdom and understanding of the word. God regrets the fact that his own children are destroyed because of lack of knowledge of him (Hosea 4:6). These are both the teachers and the students of the word. At times we may think we have known the word, yet we can still be destroyed with that knowledge. Why is this? Because the mere knowledge of the Bible without wisdom and understanding is still nothing. Knowledge not being put into use is nothing. To make this point clear ask yourself this question; How many things am I knowledgeable about and what have I done with that knowledge? In order to have better understanding about this, let's look at the worldly way of acquiring knowledge, which is education. People go to school to acquire knowledge with the aims either to get the job or to start their own business. How many people have gone to school and come away with knowledge, yet have not started their own businesses or found jobs for themselves? So, people can gain knowledge and not have the intended outcome of that knowledge. Sometimes people with knowledge acquire through education, lack jobs and may blame it on the connection and who they know to get them a job. People who have acquired this educational knowledge and not started their own business might blame it on the lack of funds. So the knowledge without people we know to help us get a job, or knowledge with a lack of funds is useless. Right. Take this example and flip it around. A literal knowledge of the Bible without wisdom and understanding is useless. It is important to know that wisdom and understanding are God's. He gives them to whom he so chooses. You cannot have wisdom and understanding without the presence of the Holy Spirit. Both wisdom and understanding are gifts of the Holy Spirt and you cannot have them without the Holy Spirit. Furthermore, the Bible for that matter was written by the Holy Spirit through his servants. If God is the author of the Bible, then who can claim to know it without God? In order to understand the Bible, the book of Ephesians 1, is critical.

Ephesians 1:17-19 That the God of our Lord Jesus Christ, the Father of glory, may give to you the spirit of wisdom and revelation in the knowledge of Him, the eyes of your understanding being enlightened; that you may know what is the hope of His calling, what are the riches of the glory of His inheritance in the saints, and what is the exceeding greatness of His power toward us who believe, according to the working of His mighty power. NJKV.

These Bible verses are so critical for the teachers and the students of the word, as it is God himself who gives us the "Spirit of wisdom," and "Spirit of revelation" to have knowledge of him. It important to note that wisdom and revelation are referred to in these verses as spirits. What does this tell you? Unless we have the Holy Spirit, we cannot have these spirits. Unless we have the permission of God to allow us to have knowledge of him, we cannot know anything about him. In the same way, you would not allow anyone to have knowledge of you without your permission. For example, wisdom allows us to apply the truth and the instructions of the gospel during our sermons. The revelation gives us deeper meanings of scriptures beyond their literal meanings, in order to have full understanding of them. Once we have this deeper revelation of scriptures, our spirits are enlightened to know what our purpose or mission on Earth are. Our main purpose for being born comes with understanding of the word of God. If we want to know why we were born, then we must read the Bible. But it is not only through reading the Bible that we may know our purpose, but also our provisions and protections. The desires of our hearts and things we would love to have in this life are given to us in the Bible.

Studying the Bible will enable us to grow in wisdom that could convict us of sin. Before our Lord Jesus Christ came to the world, the world was drowning and dying in sins. Sin of rejection of God and worshipping Satan. Once we get into the Bible it will expose our own sins. The Bible becomes the lens for seeing our own sins of lying, jealousy, envying, gossiping, bloodshed, violence, sexual immorality, injustice, greed, and corruption among others. No one who is a true follower of Jesus Christ, will deny that he or she is a sinner. The above-mentioned sins plus other sin we may be committing remotely, get admitted if we study the Bible. When we study the Bible with the help of the Holy Spirit, it truly becomes the lamp of our path and the light of our ways. Whatever we do, say and think and the way we do, say and think it becomes clearer to us. We can never stumble in light. In the book of 1 John 1, John has even put it better; *8 "If we claim to be without sin, we deceive ourselves and the truth is not in us. 9 If we confess our sins, he is faithful and just and will forgive us our sins and purify us from all unrighteousness. 10 If we claim we have not sinned, we make him out to be a liar and his word is not in us."*

Studying the Bible make us good teachers of the word. Training and teaching the word is a huge task that needs the help of the Holy Spirit. If we as teachers of the word, are to be equipped in teaching the word then we must study the Bible.

2 Timothy 3: 16 All Scripture is given by inspiration of God, and is profitable for doctrine, for reproof, for correction, for instruction in righteousness, 17 that the man of God may be complete, thoroughly equipped for every good work. NKJV.

The Bible is given to us purposely for our life on Earth. We must live, think and work by it. As Christians, everything that we do must be based on the Bible. You see everything we do in this life is based on our own thoughts, words, and actions or the advice of others. But what is the basis or the anchor of our own actions? They are all based on our own, beliefs, character traits, values, knowledge, wisdom and understanding. What about if we left them aside and relied on God's, beliefs, values, and character traits found in the Bible?

According to the Bible verse above, the Bible is profitable for doctrine to teach. For the teachers of the word, the Bible is actually the curriculum where we can plan our teachable topic of our choice. The doctrines for example about the sins and repentance of sins, baptism, Christ's birth, death and resurrection, truth, righteousness, faithfulness, the creation of the world, eternal life, Christ as the head of the church. These plus many others are the doctrines that we need to teach to our hearers and followers. Everything we teach must be about the Kingdom of God and the salvation of mankind from their sin. For example, today there are many false teachers of the word who will never talk about sin, yet it is the very reason why Christ came to the world. But not only that, it is the reason why we were separated from God in the first place due to the rebellion of Adam. Today the same sin continues to separate us from God if we reject our lord Jesus Christ and his gospel of salvation.

The Bible is also the source with which we can correct our own heresies and errors. There are many heresies today in the world and if we lack knowledge of the Bible we can easily be deceived or misled. For example, one of those heresies is the belief that Christ has died for our sins, and we are forgiven and going to heaven. It is true that Christ has indeed died for our sins, but we cannot continue to live a sinful lifestyle. There is no way you can continue to live a sinful lifestyle and expect to go to heaven. Before you became a Christian you were not conscious of your sin, but when you became a Christian, you became conscious of your sins. The moment you became conscious of your sin and repented; you were forgiven. But not if you continue to commit sin willingly and wilfully. When you commit sin knowing that it is wrong to do so and with your full knowledge of its consequences, then you cannot be forgiven. That falls under God's judgment, because you are testing God. Furthermore, there are many teachers of the word, who have come out in support of abortion, same sex marriage, and gender changes, yet it unlawful in the Bible. Marriage in the Bible is between one man and one woman.

Any other marriage is against the doctrine of Christ. If these other marriages were good, God himself would have told us in the Bible. If any marriage is not in the Bible, then it is an error that needs to be avoided, condemned, and rejected in all churches of Christ.

When we study the Bible, we can correct ourselves. When failed to admit our own sins then one else filled by the Holy Spirit can tell us about them. In the world we live in today it has become very difficult to correct people. It is inherent within human beings to resist any correction that points out their mistakes. If we as teachers of the word must correct people, then it must be based on the word of God. It is important to note that before we bring correction, we must also be careful and conscious of our own mistakes. You cannot correct a person with the same mistakes and wrongdoings you are committing. Remember the big plank is always in our eyes and the speck, in other people's eyes (Mathew 7:5). Furthermore, correction must also be done in love. Never point out sins of others and disown or fail to forgive them. Correction is to improve, not to make the already bad situation worse by our correction. We must be cautious of the way we speak to people. That's why when we teach, we must allow the Holy Spirit to speak through us. We must be kind and gentle with and to each other.

Let me tell you my own personal experiential testimony about correction. My personal position on abortion is that it is a sin, and it must not be done. One day I came across a gentleman at my workplace, who had authorised his girlfriend to kill their unborn child through abortion. In the conversation I was speaking strongly and randomly against abortion and why it should not be done. As soon as I said abortion is an evil act, and a person who has committed one is guilty of sin, the gentleman broke down in tears. I was caught by surprise and without words I stood speechlessly before him waiting to hear and explain to me what has gone wrong in our conversation. As soon as he stopped crying, he spoke to me in a broken voice telling me, how he had authorised his girlfriend to get the abortion and now he is guilty of killing his unborn child. He continued that his girlfriend was not able to be a good mother to the child, because she was a drug addict, cutting herself every day and throwing herself on the floor while pregnant. With his justification of abortion and the emotions that accompanied it, I was terrified and shaking all over my body, thinking about how to get out of his presence let alone correct him of his wrongdoing. After a while of silence, all I said to him was I was sorry for bringing up such an offensive conversation. I went further and told him, there are many reasons such as sickness, medical complications and incest, as to why people undergo an authorised abortion. As soon as he heard me speak about these reasons why people committed abortions, his guilty conscience was relieved. And the conversation ended. There was no correction here, instead I ended up supporting his position on abortion, in order to comfort him.

Although what the gentleman had done is a crime against the unborn child, I had no place telling him, because my approach was wrong. I had held a random conversation without being mindful of the fact that the person I spoke to could be one of them. I spoke without having explored the advantages and disadvantages of speaking against abortion publicly and openly to people. The simple takeaway in this is that correction must done in careful and gentle ways that are free of judgement and criticism of people.

My approach would have been different had I known about his authorisation of the abortion of his unborn child. First, of all I would have been careful with my language, judgement and criticism of people who have committed the sin of abortion. If I knew the gentleman had committed the sin of abortion, I would have focused more on the sin of abortion than the person who has committed abortion. We must not speak in a way that turns away people who have committed sin. In fact, Christ came for the sinners that they may be saved. If sinners don't get saved through our messages, then we have violated Christ's doctrine of correction with love. That is why, as teachers of the Bible, we must be under the training of the Holy Spirit.

RECEIVING: BIBLE

When you have prayed and are expecting God to answer your prayers, the Bible is the best source of your answered prayers. The Bible is full of previous prayed and answered prayers of great men and women of God. You can look at how they prayed and how their prayers were answered, and how those prayers pertain to your areas of interests for which you are praying. At times God may choose to answer our prayers very quickly or he may choose to delay them as a matter of his choice. But it is important to note even if your prayers are answered or delayed it is all for your best interests. Some prayers may be quickly answered by God to grow our faith, or some prayers may be delayed for our training, or some prayers may be delayed due to God's timing. Our Lord knows what is good for us in the end. The mistake we may make at times when our prayers are delayed, is to quit in the middle while the living God is preparing for us a better outcome. Remember our prayers must be within God's will for us. Let us look at a great man of God, who prayed in the Bible and how God answered his prayers. And this was none other than the prophet Elijah at Mount Carmel.

1 Kings 18:36-40 And it came to pass, at the time of the offering of the evening sacrifice, that Elijah the prophet came near and said, "Lord God of Abraham, Isaac, and Israel, let it be known this day that You are God in Israel and I am Your servant, and that I have done all these things at Your word. Hear me, O Lord, hear me, that this people may know that You are the Lord God, and that You have turned their hearts back to You again." Then the fire of the Lord fell and consumed the burnt sacrifice, and the wood and the stones and the dust, and it licked up the water that was in the trench. Now when all the people saw it, they fell on their faces; and they said, "The Lord, He is God! The Lord, He is God!" And Elijah said to them, "Seize the prophets of Baal! Do not let one of them escape!" So they seized them; and Elijah brought them down to the Brook Kishon and executed them there. NKJV.

In these verses we can see how Elijah prayed to God and how God responded immediately. There was a problem of idol worship in Israel that the prophet Elijah confronted. Ahab and his wife Jezebel had turned the people of Israel into idol worshippers. But as if that is not enough, Jezebel persecuted the people of God. Most of the people of God were either killed or scattered to other nations fearing for their lives. What did idol worship cause in Israel? It caused confusion, division, lying, killing, adultery, stealing, oppression of widows, orphans and poor, bloodshed, violence, and all forms of injustice. God was not happy about what was happening among his people, and he had raised up a prophet who confronted it. The prayers of Elijah were within God's "will," not only for him but the nation of Israel. Look at how he prayed; "***Lord God of Abraham, Isaac, and Israel, let it be known this day that You are God in Israel, and I am Your servant, and that I have done all these things at Your word. Hear me, O Lord, hear me, that this people may know that You are the Lord God, and that You have turned their hearts back to You again.***"

In his prayers, Elijah acknowledged God as a God of his ancestors, the only true God of Israel and himself as his servant who acted on his word. Although the Bible has not given us in detail how Elijah spoke with God to bring up the contest between him and the nine hundred fifty prophets of Baal and Asherah, it was an instruction from God to do so, in order to return the children of Israel to himself as the true God that deserves to be worship. He goes further; "**Hear me, O Lord, hear me, that this people may know that You are the Lord God, and that You have turned their hearts back to You again.**" God responded to Elijah's prayer because he is the true God that needs to be worshipped and only, he could turn the people's hearts to himself from idol worship. He knows what is in a human being's heart and he could change it for good if people repent and cry out to him. It is important to note that God will never do anything unless we have partnered with him.

Do people have the same problems of idol worship today in nations? If so, then what are the servants of the Lord doing about it? Certainly, they do and I will talk about my own country of South Sudan. In South Sudan we have crossed the line by offering human sacrifices to idols for example, we have today in South Sudan, in Shilluk kingdom, where two contestants for the leadership are sent underwater, and one must remain under water, and one resurface back. The one that resurfaces back is believed to be the one chosen by NyiKaag to lead the Shilluk kingdom for life. The winner of the contested leadership is entitled therefore to enjoy all the privileges and rights that come with it such as wealth, power, honour, glory, and strength.

It is not only in the Kingdom of Shilluk alone one can see this demonic control of the country. Across the nation of South Sudan in towns and villages you can see many symbols of idol worship either in people's wrists, arms, waists and cuttings of human bodies, places, shrines, temples, spears and spear masters, beads, water and water points, animals and plants. Furthermore, you can see magicians, sorcerers, diviners, astrologers, and spell casters working and confessing openly as devil worshipers. They promise their victims wealth, longlife, husbands and wives, power, fame, and employment and so much more. But all of these are lies from the pit of hell. The Bible is very clear; the devil comes to steal, kill and destroy (John 10:10). In fact, these lies of Satan have caused too much suffering to the people of South Sudan. Across the nation today there is violence everywhere, bloodshed, injustice, sexual immortality, greed, and corruption; these are all the works of the devil that the Prophet Elijah had to confront in Israel.

Now is the time for the Elijah's of South Sudan to rise and challenge the Satanic hegemony in South Sudan. It is only God who can rescue the country from the hands of wicked human beings. The religious leaders must preach the uncensored and unfiltered word of God to the people of the nation. Not only is the gospel the good news of salvation, but it also has ability to convict people of their sins to stop worshipping the devil. The problem of the nation normally comes from people influenced by Satan to do wrong over good. If you want to change the nation, then you must change the people's beliefs, ways and thinking in order to do good.

On a personal level, you can use the Bible, by quoting the scriptures against the devil, in order to defeat him. ***James 4:7 Therefore submit to God. Resist the devil and he will flee from you.* NKJV.** The first thing you must do before you can resist the devil is to submit to God. The Devil is not our match, and we cannot fight or resist him without the presence of God with us. We must be first baptised with the baptism of water (for our sins) and the baptism of the Holy Spirit (to live inside us). When we have repented of our sins then the devil has no legal rights over us, and the Holy Spirit can come and live inside us. When these two things happen then you will have a better chance of resisting the devil. We can now intensify our resistance through our prayers, fasting, reading and reciting the word of God. The only force the devil cannot withstand is the word of God. You must pray while quoting the scriptures against the devil, in order to defeat him using the word. For example, if you have a sickness in your body and you want the healing in your body then go to the Bible and look for verses or a verse about that sickness that you want to be free from and quote that verse against the sickness and you will see it leave your body.

Blessings and prosperity are God's. Not only is the Bible a

book to study in order to improve our knowledge, wisdom, and understanding of God, but it is also a book full of heavenly blessings of our God the father. All our provisions, protection and assignments are in the Bible. Given the fact that God is the father for us all, what he has done for one of his children in the past he will do it again for his current children including you. The mistake people make is to exclude themselves from the provisions of God. The same God who fed five thousand people with five loaves of bread and two fish, will do it again today. The same God who let the manna rained from heaven and let quails gathered in the evening around the camp of the, Hebrews, will do it again today for us. The same God who sustained the Widow of Zarephath with a little flour and oil in a jar will do it again today for us.

The Bible is the source of endurance and encouragement. When we suffer, we endure it with hope and joy that God will see us through it. This brings encouragement to our bodies, souls and spirits. There are many seasons under the sun. There are times for peace, love and joy and there are times of disappointment, stress, fear, anger, depression. But he that suffers knowing that God is with him, endures to the end. God has not hidden this fact from us. He said, In the world you have many troubles, but be cheerful because have overcome the world. If we go through many troubles knowing that God is with us, then we can easily overcome them. Because of the things we suffer we can be comforted by God, in order to comfort those who may go through the same suffering in the future. God gives us strength in our weakness. This is to prove to us that we cannot be independent of God, but dependent on him.

Faith comes by hearing, and hearing by the word of God.

There is no way we can have faith unless we study and hear the word of God being preached to us. The word of God can develop our faith in God. Remember, the just shall live by faith. Because without faith we cannot please God. I always say that faith is our bank card we can used to withdraw our provisions from God. Our faith will be highly developed if we take time to study the word of God. If we go to the Bible, we will learn more about great men and women of God who had great faith, that not only pleased God but he also enabled them to overcome their conditions. The salvation of our souls can only be obtained through our faith and the same for other things we want God to do for us. Peter says the trials we go through are to show the genuineness of our faith for salvation. Those things we suffer and overcome give us confidence in the God we serve and the battles we can win through him.

VOICE

No single human being on this planet would deny the fact that God has spoken to them at least on one occasion. He would have done it through the Bible or through his servants the Prophets, Apostles, or Priests. As if that is not enough, he has done it through his beautiful creation. Everything on this planet speaks to us about the God we cannot see with our own eyes. Everything on this planet carries the voice of God whether living or non-living things. We are liars if we think he doesn't. Ask yourself this question and see how you will answer it; Who created all these around me? For example, the people, animals and plants, oceans and seas, sun, moon and stars and other non-living thing, the mountains, gold, bronze and silver and precious stones. Well as far as the world is concerned no one has claimed the creation of these things on Earth and in the heavens apart from God himself. It is only in the Bible that you can learn the claim and the ownership of these things by God himself.

Psalm 50:7 "Hear, O My people, and I will speak, O Israel, and I will testify against you; I am God, your God! 8 I will not rebuke you for your sacrifices Or your burnt offerings, Which are continually before Me. 9 I will not take a bull from your house, Nor goats out of your folds. 10 For every beast of the forest is Mine, And the cattle on a thousand hills. 11 I know all the birds of the mountains, And the wild beasts of the field are Mine. 12 "If I were hungry, I would not tell you; For the world is Mine, and all its fullness. 13 Will I eat the flesh of bulls, Or drink the blood of goats? 14 Offer to God thanksgiving, And pay your vows to the Most High. 15 Call upon Me in the day of trouble; I will deliver you, and you shall glorify Me." NKJV.

This is very amazing, who else can claim the creation of these things apart from God himself? Let him come up and do so. This is the question, and every human being must answer including yourself. Furthermore, in verse 15 above, he has even invited us to call on him in our days of trouble in order to deliver us from our troubles. He is saying, call me at the times of your troubles and I will deliver for you to glorify me. I will bet you who has no troubles of his own on Earth right now not to call out to God, in order not to be set free. I don't know about you, but I do. Another challenge to you and me today, have you tried to call him, to see whether he will respond? If you haven't then this is your chance today to call out to the Lord God of heaven and Earth. It is astounding that many people on Earth today just conclude that there is no God without calling on him first.

God does speak unless you are not his sheep. It is our Lord Jesus Christ who said this. God does speak unless you have denied his existence. God does speak unless you haven't prayed. God does speak unless you haven't read the Bible.

***John 10:1 "Most assuredly, I say to you, he who does not enter the sheepfold by the door, but climbs up some other way, the same is a thief and a robber. 2 But he who enters by the door is the shepherd of the sheep. 3 To him the doorkeeper opens, and the sheep hear his voice; and he calls his own sheep by name and leads them out.* NKJV.**

Christ himself has declared here that he is the true shepherd, who can only be heard by his sheep, and he can lead them. Like I said earlier, unless you are the sheep of Christ you will never hear his voice. Furthermore, not only is Christ the shepherd of sheep, but he is also the way, truth and the life. If Christ is the way to God, then there is no way we can hear God's voice unless we accept Christ and allow him to live inside of us. He that climbs up the sheepfold, Jesus declared him as thief and robber. Anyone that preaches about God yet fails to acknowledge that Christ has come in the flesh, is not of God. He has the spirit of antichrist, and you will never hear God's voice through him. The self-appointed Pharisees, Sadducees and scribes and today's false teachers, prophets and apostles are thieves and robbers who climb up the sheepfold and not by the door. Christ is the only true shepherd appointed by God to lead us to himself and we can hear his voice and follow him. By God's commission, authority and power, he was sent to the Earth by God, and he has redeemed us by his blood and flesh and restored us back to God. Although, we can hear the voice of Christ through his gospel ministers, and the Holy Spirit, Christ makes himself known to his believers. This is an assurance that if two or three of us gather in his name he promised to be in our midst. If we hear and keep the commandments of God, Christ will manifest himself to us. There is no better example of this pledge of his manifestation than that one of St Paul on his way to Damascus, where he heard Christ's voice and instruction of what to do. St Paul had one encounter with Christ, and it changed his life forever. Christ became real to St Paul and since that time going forward, he never doubted his existence. This encounter plus many others are good examples of hearing God's voice. The death of Christ and his resurrection has given us the Holy Spirit who lives inside us. Today we don't need Prophets and Priests for God to speak to us. With the help of the Holy Spirit, we can speak to God directly.

Again, three things are critical to hearing God's voice: his creation, the Bible, and the Holy Spirit. This can be done either with help of his ministers of the gospel or through prayer, fasting and reading the Bible. No one who has taken these steps can claim to have not heard God's voice. These are the practical steps I took and with certainty, if you do the same you will hear God's voice. There is nothing in life that will give you more peace and certainty than to hear the voice of your creator. But not only that, he can help guide you in your daily decision-making, show you your true purpose, give you comfort in times of distress, and more importantly he will keep you from sinning if you know he is real.

If you haven't heard his voice or if you are struggling hearing his voice then you can take the following practical steps;

make prayer your daily lifestyle, develop the habit of reading the Bible, by laying of hands allow the Holy Spirit into your life, get a quiet time with God, and more importantly surround yourself with students and teachers of the Bible.

In as much as it is important to hear God's voice, it is also important to distinguish his voice from your own voice and that of Satan from God's. The simple rule of thumb is that your voice and God's voice, will always come from within you and Satan's voice, from outside you. Your voice will always think logically and analytically about everything. Satan's voice will always be condemning, negative, destructive, vicious, accusatory, and deceptive. His purpose is to steal, kill and destroy. Remember this always. God's voice will always be kind, peaceful, encouraging, loving, inspirational, wise, understanding, healing, knowledgeable, just, faithful, and more importantly convicting us of our wrong doings without condemning. It is important to note that God has no favourites. If I am today able to hear his voice then I can assure you, you can also hear his voice.

VISIONS AND DREAMS

The other way we can receive our answered prayers from God, is through visions and dreams. Yes, indeed I must admit that not many people can see visions but not many people can deny that they have had dreams or can dream. Dreams and visions go together, even though there are slight differences. These are a common means through which God speaks to us individually. Visions occur while we are awake and alert, while dreams occur while we are asleep. Both can occur during the day or at night, but mostly dreams happen at night.

Just as there are many people who believe in dreams and visions there are also many sceptics who do not believe them. There are many people who believe that what happens to them in visions and dreams is so important to their lives and they take it seriously. Contrastingly as well there are many people who believe that what happens to them at night in a dream or vision is not of a concern to them and they don't take it seriously. Whether you are a believer or sceptic of visions and dreams, there are merits as to why many people have arrived at those conclusions. I will not pass judgment on anyone who has done so. What I must do here is to explain, based on my own Bible knowledge and my own personal experiences why visions and dreams are important and as such we must take them seriously. Previously I must confess I was not either a believer or sceptic of visions and dreams, but I was concerned that someone or something somewhere was talking to me in a dream or vision. For example, on many occasions my own dead father would come to me in dream. I would welcome him, talk with him, we would laugh and hug each other and part ways when the dream ended. The same thing would happen to me about my dead mother as well and so many other dead people I knew in life; they would appear to me in a dream either immediately after they had died or later in life. This became a concern to me, and of course with little or no understanding of dreams and their interpretations, I became restless and terrified about such dreams.

But it is not me alone who has had such experiences. There are countless other people who have had dreams at night where they met with their loved ones who had died many years ago. Because many people, with myself included, have no clear understanding and interpretation of such dreams in the Bible, people will have many ways of explaining the dreams. For example, in my tradition among the Dinka people of South Sudan, our people believe in ancestral visitation in the night dreams. It is very interesting that they believed in life after death, way before Christians or missionaries came to Africa. The Dinka people believe that their dead ancestors can come back to them in the dream of a night either to bless them or to curse them. When this happens, and particularly if it is a life threatening or terrifying dream, the dreamer can seek answers either from dream experts within their territory or seek answers from magicians. The magicians will ask the dreamer to offer animal sacrifices to appease the death ancestors on many occasions. Apart from animal sacrifices, other rituals may be performed based on the instructions of the magicians.

The Bible is very clear, that dead people know nothing. What happened to me and other countless human beings in our dreams, was and continues to be an exploitation by the demonic spirits who, disguise themselves as our dead ancestors. For example, one of those spirits is the spirit of death. It is a deadly demon that exploits our previous relationship with our dead ancestors to come to us to steal, kill and destroy us. These demons have instructions from Satan himself to stop us from knowing God and to take away our heavenly blessings. But not only that, they have a mission to give or to plant within us sickness, deception, lying, rejection, torment, defilement, enticement, separation, poverty, jealousy, and many other evil vices. By doing this you can easily become a tool of Satan to implant his agenda on Earth. What is the takeaway from this? It is the fact that our dreams can be the source of demonic communication. Satan and his demons can talk to us in a dream. I repeat again dead people know nothing.

Ecclesiastes 9:5 For the living know that they will die; But the dead know nothing, and they have no more reward, For the memory of them is forgotten. 6 Also their love, their hatred, and their envy have now perished; Nevermore will they have a share in anything done under the sun. NKJV.

Deuteronomy 10:10 There shall not be found among you anyone who makes his son or his daughter pass through the fire, or one who practices witchcraft, or a soothsayer, or one who interprets omens, or a sorcerer, 11 or one who conjures spells, or a medium, or a spiritist, or one who calls up the dead. 12 For all who do these things are an abomination to the Lord, and because of these abominations the Lord your God drives them out from before you. 13 You shall be blameless before the Lord your God. 14 For these nations which you will dispossess listened to soothsayers and diviners; but as for you, the Lord your God has not appointed such for you. NKJV.

This begs the question, if demons can talk to us in dreams, then what about God? As we have seen in that example, I gave above about myself, our dreams can be sources of Godly or Satanic influence, and we must take them seriously. Well, I must tell you that God speaks to us through visions and dreams, and you and I must take them seriously. Take for example the case of Joseph and Mary. God spoke to them extensively through dreams and visions. Whether it was the news of the conception of our Lord Jesus Christ through Mary, or the instruction to Joseph to take him to Egypt to avoid the persecution by Herod the great, they were all communicated through visions and dreams. God knows what would have happened to our Lord

Jesus Christ had Joseph not taken seriously those instructions in the dream to take him to Egypt. These plus many other countless examples in the Bible, like that of Abraham, Jacob, Joseph, Daniel, John, Peter and St Paul, are good arguments as to why we must not take our dreams and visions lightly. In fact, we are the lucky ones, as the last generation that can enjoy dreams and visions, because we have been given the Holy Spirit. This was a pledge by God himself through the prophet Joel, (Joel 2:28), which was cited by St Peter during his sermons on the day of Pentecost, that the Lord God will pour out his Spirit on all the flesh to dream dreams and see visions.

Acts 2:17 'And it shall cone to pass in the last days, says God, That I will pour out of My Spirit on all flesh; Your sons and your daughters shall prophesy, your young men shall see visions, your old men shall dream dreams. 18 And on My menservants and on My maidservants, I will pour out My Spirit in those days; And they shall prophesy. 19 I will show wonders in heaven above and signs in the Earth beneath: Blood and fire and vapor of smoke. NKJV.

Again, the ability to dream dreams and to see visions lies today with the Holy Spirit. It is our responsibility to allow the Holy Spirit to live inside of us, for us to dream dreams and see visions. No one in the Old Testament enjoyed the advantages and the privileges of having the Holy Spirit within him, as much as Daniel. All his promotions came either because he had clear interpretation or explanations of the dreams and visions the Babylonian Kings had had, particularly Nebuchadnezzar. Nebuchadnezzar referred to Daniel as a chief of all magicians, sorcerers, astrologers, and soothsayers, because God had blessed him with understanding, knowledge, wisdom and skills of interpreting dreams and visions. The same Holy Spirit who was in Daniel, is in us today. If we yield to him and follow his instructions and guidance, we can also enjoy the same privileges and advantages Daniel had in Babylon in the business, political and social arena today. Just as Daniel had God's favour in interpreting visions and dreams, the same God can still do it today for us through the Holy Spirt. He can give us dominance in business, politics and leadership, dreams and visions that requires our interpretations and explanation to the leaders of those arenas.

However much these dreams and visions are important for us, they can sometimes get complicated, depending on who had the dream, and who interpreted the dream. It is important to note that our dreams come from either ourselves, God or Satan. There are many prophets and teachers of the Bible today, who can falsely claim to either dream dreams or interpret dreams on our behalf. The same problems that were experienced by the Old Testament prophets like Jeremiah and many others, are still being experienced today by churches and people. How do we know whether someone is making up the dreams and visions to deceive people? This is so complicated. In order to understand dreams and visions and their interpretations, two things are so critical; the Holy Spirit and the Bible. As an example, let's see what the Holy Spirit did through Daniel. God gave a dream or vision to the leaders of Babylon. God gave understanding and interpretation to Daniel, before the leaders invited their magicians, astrologers and soothsayers. After they failed to explain the dreams and visions Daniel was invited to bring an interpretation. Daniel was able to immediately and exactly explain the meaning of the dreams and visions to the leaders. What does this mean today? God will give us clear understanding and interpretations of dreams and visions. But not only that, such dreams and visions will also align with the Bible. If you have a dream or vision you can go to the Bible and find the meaning. This is the rule of thumb; if it is not in the Bible then you can discard such a dream or vision. God is not a liar and if what is claimed to be a prophetic dream or vision by the prophet does not come to pass, then that prophet is a liar, and you don't have to believe them.

More importantly, dreams and visions are also sources from which we can receive our assignment from God. How many people have dreamed dreams, where God has spoken to them clearly about their vision and mission on Earth?

Job 33:14 For God may speak in one way, or in another, yet man does not perceive it. 15 In a dream, in a vision of the night, when deep sleep falls upon men, while slumbering on their beds, 16 Then He opens the ears of men, And seals their instruction. 17 In order to turn man from his deed, and conceal pride from man, 18 He keeps back his soul from the Pit, And his life from perishing by the sword. NKJV.

These are wonderful verses from the book of Job, about our dreams and visions. Not only does God speak to us through dreams and visions to give us our assignments, but he also gives us instructions that keeps us away from sinning. The saddest thing according to Job is the fact that people don't take their dreams and visions seriously, including the dreams that can save them from sin and death and thereafter hell. The night visions and dreams are still the major ways God speaks to us today after we have retired to our beds, with no more conversations and distractions. This is because during the day we are distracted by our work, families, friends and studies, and have less focus on what God is communicating to us.

Dreams and visions are important for people and nations today as God continues to communicate to us what needs to be done. The direction and the vision of the country and her people need the prophets who can hear from God. We must learn to write down our dreams and visions and ask God to give us interpretation of them through the help of the Holy Spirit, or Pastors or other people who have better understanding and interpretation of dreams and visions. As shown in the Bible verse I have shared above, never take your dreams and vision lightly; the are major sources through which God still speaks to us today. Dreams and visions can help us know our agenda or can help us avoid disaster.

WORD OF KNOWLEDGE

Word of knowledge is specific information given to us by the Holy Spirit about certain things or about conditions of the person. The Holy Spirit will give us this information that we wouldn't have with our natural knowledge. Depending on the need of the person, the word of knowledge could be about the loss of items, healing, danger, a crisis, job, marriage, contract, or thoughts within the person's mind. This could be about the person's past, present or future event that the Holy Spirit is trying to educate us about.

The word of knowledge is made known to you by the Holy Spirit through "inner knowing." Many may not agree with this, but it does happen to us all even to the non-believers. It can come in the Forms of a thought, impression on your mind, vision, or picture in your mind. Those who are filled with the presence of the Holy Spirit know this. When the Holy Spirit speaks through the person, he speaks the same way the person speaks to us from outside. Let me give you my practical example. There was one day I had lost my car keys. I searched and I couldn't find my keys for a while until I made a conclusion that I must ask the Holy Spirit. And I said, "Lord Holy Spirit show me my keys." He spoke to me to go into the garage and open my car and I would find them there. I did exactly according to his instructions, and I found my keys in the car. What a wonderful thing to be a friend of the Holy Spirit. He is our helper, and he can help us in every condition or situation. Many people will doubt this, so let us go into the Bible to see where and who used the word of knowledge extensively.

No one used the word of knowledge about people or things more than our Lord Jesus Christ. Whether it was Peter's denial of him three times, whether it was Peter rebuking him about his crucifixion, and how he responded by saying Get behind me Satan, whether it was Judas Iscariot's betrayal of him, whether it was seeing and telling Nathaniel about him sitting under the fig tree before they met, whether it was the Pharisees being indignant about his healing on the Sabbath, whether it was a predicting his death and resurrection in the third day, or many other examples, he would instantly know this information within himself. All of these are evidence of the use of word of knowledge by him.

John 1:47 Jesus saw Nathanael coming toward Him, and said of him, "Behold, an Israelite indeed, in whom is no deceit!" 48 Nathanael said to Him, "How do You know me?" Jesus answered and said to him, "Before Philip called you, when you were under the fig tree, I saw you." 49 Nathanael answered and said to Him, "Rabbi, you are the Son of God! You are the King of Israel!" 50 Jesus answered and said to him, "Because I said to you, 'I saw you under the fig tree,' do you believe? You will see greater things than these." NKJV.

John 4: 16 Jesus said to her, "Go, call your husband, and come here." 17 The woman answered and said, "I have no husband." Jesus said to her, "You have well said, 'I have no husband,' 18 for you have had five husbands, and the one whom you now have is not your husband; in that you spoke truly." 19 The woman said to Him, "Sir, I perceive that You are a prophet. NKJV.

It is important to note that if you are blessed with this gift then you must use it wisely to help yourself and others. There is a danger associated with this gift and one must exercise high standards of conscientiousness because there is risk involved with knowing people's information. God gifts us this ability to help people, not to destroy them. The information you have about people must not be shared with friends or any other people. People are entitled to their privacy even if you have their information with you.

2 Peter 1:5 But also for this very reason, giving all diligence, add to your faith virtue, to virtue knowledge, 6 to knowledge self-control, to self-control perseverance, to perseverance godliness, 7 to godliness brotherly kindness, and to brotherly kindness love. 8 For if these things are yours and abound, you will be neither barren nor unfruitful in the knowledge of our Lord Jesus Christ. NKJV.

PROPHECY

God communicates with the prophets through the voice, visions and dreams, word of knowledge, and many signs and wonders they receive from God and declare to the people. The office of prophecy deals with future events only, as God shows the prophets what will happen in the future in society. The office of prophetic deals with a person, people, communities, societies and nations in the foretelling of their future by God through the prophets. It is important to note that in the Old Testament, God used to speak to people through the prophets by the Holy Spirit. In fact, God declared it himself through the prophet Amos, that he can do nothing unless he reveals it to his servants the prophets.

Amos 3:7 Surely the Lord God does nothing, unless He reveals His secret to His servants the prophets. **NKJV.**

Well, that was the Old Testament, but today God speaks and reveals things to us all through the Holy Spirit who lives in us all. It is the Holy Spirit who declares to us the deep things of God. It is the role of the Holy Spirit to tell us things to come. Many people today still believe to hear the word of prophecy through the prophets and not the Holy Spirit who is within them. As soon as you are baptised with the Holy Spirit, nothing can stop you from hearing the word of prophecy through the Holy Spirit who is within you. This word of prophecy can be for you or other people. This is not to undermine the prophets and the office of prophecy. God still raises up prophets today, through whom he speaks. Prophecy is the gift of the Holy Spirit, and he can give it to whom he chooses. He gave some to be prophets, apostles, evangelists, pastors and teachers, purposely for the equipping and edification of the saints. All you need to do is to practice hearing the voice of the Holy Spirit and you will be right. The reason many people are deceived today is because they are chasing after the word of prophecy from the prophets, some of whom may not be true prophets. Rather you must chase after the Holy Spirit, than the prophets. If you desire anything from God, including the gift of prophecy, then God can readily give to you.

God still speaks to us today through the prophets. So far so good, but what is very controversial is; Who among the prophets does God speak through to us? Who among the prophets declares the word of God to us as it was given? Who among the prophets lie to us out of the fantasy that they speak to God? Who among the prophets is being used by the Devil to lie to us about our future? Stay with me now as we distinguish them here.

WHO ARE THE TRUE PROPHETS?

True prophets of God are God's spokes people on the behalf of him. God trusts them and they trust God. True prophets of God receive the word of God and declare it to us as it is given by God to us, and which must come to pass. The true prophets of God acknowledge-the "Holy Spirit", as the power behind the miracles they perform and the words of inspiration they give to us. And more importantly, the true prophets of God condemn human sins in individuals, communities, societies and nations. What they say must come to pass. What they say is to correct the sinful nature of people and not to condemn them. Prophecies are for hope and not despair. Prophecies are for correction not judgement and condemnation. In the New Testament dispensation, judgment and condemnation have been exclusively given to Christ and not the prophets.

WHO ARE THE FALSE PROPHETS?

False prophets are self-proclaimed prophets, who claim to hear the word from God, and speak the word to the people. False prophets can also be defined as people who claim the gift of prophecy or divine inspiration to speak for God, yet they are under the influence of the Devil. The Devil shows them misguided visions and dreams that do not come to pass or if they do, then there must strings attached, to it, like payment of money and selling of your soul. False prophets will point people to themselves, other gods, and to theories aimed at deviating people away from the true God of Heaven. False prophets will never condemn human sins as they themselves live lives of sin. As we have seen in the bible, false prophets and false prophecy is not a thing of the recent past but have existed through human history. False prophets, whether they are under the influence of the Devil or they do it out of their fantasy, have the following motivations: desire for power, influence, control, prestige, money and sexual desires. All of these have been given to us by God and you don't need to give someone money to receive them. If you lack any of the above, then you must first seek the Kingdom of God and they must be given to you. Why do you have to pay anybody for the things God has given you. Why pay anything, because Christ paid the price for you to have them. We can never buy our miracles from God.

Jeremiah 28:15 Then the prophet Jeremiah said to Hananiah

the prophet, "Hear now, Hananiah, the Lord has not sent you, but you make this people trust in a lie. 16 Therefore thus says the Lord: 'Behold, I will cast you from the face of the Earth. This year you shall die, because you have taught rebellion against the Lord.' " 17 So Hananiah the prophet died the same year in the seventh month. NKJV.

Supported by the above verses of the bible, it is crystal clear that false prophets are doing one thing – pulling people away from God, by getting them to believe in a lie. God is never a liar, and anyone who makes the people of God believe and trust the lie, has committed a punishable offense against God. Liars fit the description of the devil. And indeed, their source of power is either from the demons or themselves. They are all interested in getting power, wealth, prestige and popularity that make them feel good and look good in the eyes of people. Lying on behalf of God has a deadly consequence, as we have seen in the case of Hananiah, against Jeremiah. God killed Hananiah for lying to the people of Israel. He presented himself to the people of Israel against the prophet Jeremiah as the true prophet of God, yet he was a liar, who was never sent by God. Anybody who lies on behalf of God, can be proven wrong by God himself. Besides that, if what they say does not come to pass then you know that they are lying on behalf of God. They are nothing but agents of the devil himself.

Christians have the responsibility to accept and hold fast to what is true and deny what is false. We must also be vigilant to those prophets and teachers as to whether they acknowledge the Holy Spirit, Jesus Christ and God as the only way for your salvation. We must stick to our bible as a guideline for what we think, speak and do in order not to be lost at these defining moments of the end time. Focus on hearing the Holy Spirit within your innermost being and you will see the move of God within you.

LAW OF CONSCIENCE

The world calls it the law of nature and we in the kingdom of God, call it the law of God. The law of conscience is the ability to judge between what is right and what is wrong, within oneself. The law of conscience is embedded within human nature, whether a person is civilised or uncivilised, educated, or uneducated. All men and women have the law of conscience within their Spirits. Not a single person on this planet can deny the fact that before they do right or wrong, they could choose before they ever commit one over the other. If you choose right over wrong, then you have obeyed the law of conscience, but if you choose wrong over right then you have broken the law of conscience.

This law of conscience is written by God himself in people's hearts as part of keeping people way from sinning, and to prepare them for salvation. Before Christ came on the scene, natural laws were written on stone but when Christ came and died for us, the natural laws were now written in people's hearts purposely for our salvation. This law will give man and woman the ability to know that they are sinning before they sin. Before you lie you will know way before that you are lying before you steal you will know way before you stole before you kill you will know way that you are going to kill. Whether you sin or not, now depends on how you rule your conscience. A man or a woman with pure conscience practises love, peace, joy, righteousness, truth with all people and in all situations and conditions. Whereas a man or a woman with an impure conscience, practises lying, division, racism, discrimination, dishonesty, cheating, adultery, corruption, greed, injustice among others under all conditions and all situations.

Hebrews 10:16 "This is the covenant that I will make with them after those days, says the Lord: I will put My laws into their hearts, and in their minds, I will write them," 17 then He adds, "Their sins and their lawless deeds I will remember no more." 18 Now where there is remission of these, there is no longer an offering for sin. NKJV.

For mankind to live righteously on Earth, the law of conscience must be in play. Before Christ came into the world all people were beastly, with no ability to judge between what is right or wrong. Even though they knew what is right from what is wrong, there was no basis of judging it. When the law of Moses came, humanity's nature was already corrupted by sin. People were willingly committing sin without a second thought because the law of conscience was not written in their hearts. Today the obligation to live a peaceful life, freedom to have justice and association, right to life, marriage, and to own properties and to do common good for society are first guaranteed to us in our hearts by the law of conscience, given to us by God. That is why they are referred to as natural laws by nations. Natural laws are God given to humanity.

Now the gospel of our lord Jesus Christ is good news to all people on Earth. The ability to awaken our consciences to do the right from wrong is awakened within us by the word of God. I will here give my own example. Before I became a Christian, I had the ability to judge between what is right and wrong, but I had no duty or obligation to choose and to do the right over wrong. And this did not apply to me alone. It applies to every single person. One may be fully aware of right and wrong, but one may not choose right from wrong. Now that we have known God's law of conscience through the gospel, we have the responsibility, duty and obligation to perform it. The Bible refers to us as children of light because we have known the truth about God's law and what is expected of us to do it. The way you can do the right thing is to have its knowledge and know its consequences. Without the knowledge of truth there can never be faith and progression in doing good towards God.

Without the knowledge of law conscience and its consequences, the human "will" is a dangerous weapon that can overrule your ability to judge between what is right and wrong every single time. A human "will" that is connected to self-righteousness and self-will can easily overrule our consciousness in every single decision we make, whether right or wrong. That is why God gave us the Holy Spirit as our helper to guide us to all the truth and to help us in our decision making. Human "will", and human "emotions" can only be controlled by the Holy Spirit, for us not to sin. The law of conscience is certain, and it can give us the ability to judge between what is right or wrong without committing any error or sin. The person who exercises the law of conscience will always act truthfully and morally within himself and others around him. We have a duty and obligation to apply the law of conscience in every decision-making process in our life. The law of conscience is above the code of conduct, rule and regulations, civil and criminal laws, and anyone who exercises it can never fall into the trap of natural world laws. We wholeheartedly thank our lord

Jesus Christ for enabling us to have this gift of the Holy Spirit to be our guide in all matters of our lives, at least for those of us who believe in him.

BIBLIOGRAPHY

Anderson, Neil T. 2019. The Bondage Breaker; Overcoming negative thoughts, irrational feelings, and habitual sins. Oregon: Harvest House Publishers.

Bradley, Michael. 2020. Bible Knowledge. 18 December. Accessed January 23, 2021.https://www.bible-knowledge.com.

Bray, Claudine. 2013. Hope and Healings my True Story. San Giovanni Teatino: Evangelista Media.

George, Malkmus, Peter, and Stowe Shockey. 2006. The Hallelujah Diet; Experience the optimal health you were meant to have. Shippensburg, PA: Destiny Image.

Hernandez, David Diga. 2016. 25 Truths about Demons and Spiritual Warfare. Florida: Charisma House.

Hedland, Leif. 2017. Giant Slayers. Shippensburg, PA: Destiny Image. Johnson, Beni. 2015. Healthy and Free. Shippensburg: Destiny Image.

Leaf, Dr Caroline. 2016. Think and Eat Yourself Smart. Michigan: Baker Publishing Group.

McIntosh, Ron. 2017. The missing ingredient: Discover the one thing that changes everything. Santa Anna, CA: Trilogy Christian Publishing.

Munroe, Dr Myles. 2012. Reclaiming God' s Original Purpose for your Life. Shippensburg: Destiny Image.

Stambaugh, James. 2000. Blue Letter Bible. 1 January. Accessed June 26, 2021. https://www.blueletterbible.org.

Tripp, Paul David. 2011. Forever; Why You cannot Live without it. Michigan: Zondervan.

Willard, Dallas. 2006. Revolution of Character. Hampshire: Ashford Colour Press.

Womack, Andrew. 2021. Citizen heaven. 22 June. Accessed June 26, 2021. https://citizenheaven.wordpress.com.

D'Alessandro, Lauren. 2013. "Armour of God." The you are project 1.

Evans, Tony. 2011. Victory in Spiritual Warfare. Oregon: Harvest House Publishers. 2021. Face forward Columbus. 8 March. Accessed March 8, 2021. https://faceforwardcolumbus.com.

Prince, Derek. 2015. Blessing or Curse. London: Derek Prince Ministries UK.

Renner, Rick. 2015. Dressed to Kill. Pennsylvania: Harrison House Publishers.

Rose. 2021. "Christian Book Corporation." Christian Book Corporation Web Site. 3 March. Accessed March 3, 2021. https://www.christianbook.com.

Stewart, Don. 2021. "Introducing the case for Christianity." Blue letter bible 1.

HOW TO CONNECT WITH US:

The Life in the Spirit Ministry.
Perth, Western Australia, Australia.

Facebook.com / The Life in the Spirit ministry

Youtube.com / The Life in the Spirit ministry

www.ingramcontent.com/pod-product-compliance
Lightning Source LLC
Chambersburg PA
CBHW030253010526
44107CB00053B/1691